For Truth's Sake

for TRUTH'S sake

*R*estoring a PASSION *for* TRUTH to the people of God

NEIL SILVERBERG

MASTER PRESS

Published by Master Press

FOR TRUTH'S SAKE
Restoring a Passion for Truth to the People of God

published by Master Press

© 2010 by Neil Silverberg
All rights reserved
Cover design by Kim Taylor (kimiweb.com)

Printed in the United States

FOR TRUTH'S SAKE
Restoring a Pasion for Truth to the People of God
ISBN 978-0-9790296-5-3

For information:
MASTER PRESS
318 S.E. 4TH TERRACE • CAPE CORAL, FL

Mail to: publishing@ masterpressbooks.com

To
Micah, Joel and David
May you be lovers of the truth

Contents

Acknowledgements

Readers often tire of the habit of authors to acknowledge their spouses and children at the beginning of their works. Yet authors have good reason for doing so. The exorbitant amount of time it takes to write a book means that family members have inevitably made enormous sacrifices. For that reason writers feel obligated to mention them in their acknowledgments. I will not bother to dispense with this practice.

To begin with, this work would not have been possible without the love and full support of my wife, Shelly. As lover, partner, counselor, and consoler, she excels. For over thirty years she has stood by my side allowing me the freedom to pursue all that God has called me to be and do. I am thankful to a loving Father for his kind provision of such a life partner.

Numerous saints have encouraged me in this work without whom I would not have had the courage to finish it. Thanks Steve and Mark and Pete and Oz and the entire Masterbuilders team for your encouragement along the way. Thanks to all the assemblies in Masterbuilders as well who allowed me to teach these things in their pulpits and who responded so encouragingly when I first shared the idea for this book. And thanks Sheila for all the many hours you spent pouring over this manuscript.

Most of all, I thank my God for the privilege of being occupied with these things over the entire writing process. While getting them on paper was not easy, I thoroughly enjoyed the process. May all who read these words know the delight that I have known in the writing of them. Amen

Foreword

While this book has been several years forthcoming, I have lived with its message for most of my life. In preaching, teaching, writing, and personal counseling, my life's goal has been to help people come alive to Jesus Christ through the written Word. That's where I first met Him, and where I continue to find all of the resources needed for life and ministry. So it is quite natural that I would write a book about how to discover Him in the Word.

Finding time to do so, though, has not been easy. This book was written during the busiest period of my life and ministry. Between preaching, pastoral ministry, increased travel and my work as an editor for other authors, I have literally had to fight tooth and nail to find time to write it. Most of it was written on airplanes, in coffee shops, airports, and wherever I happened to have a few minutes. I doubt that there was a single chapter written in one place. Much of it was written at various Dunkin' Donuts (thank God for the #2).

While there were many things contributing to this work, by far my primary motivation has been the increasing subjectivism which compels many of God's people to seek after experiences with God without submitting them to the scrutiny of Scripture. This subjectivism has produced a caricature of the passionate Christian as a person *mainly* concerned with experiences rather than the Word of God. While I preached the majority of the content of this work in sermons in various church pulpits, it was hearing a message by Pastor Dave Harvey of Philadelphia entitled, *The Subjective Captivity of the Church* which gave me the needed encouragement to believe this book needed to be written.

Authors rarely feel their books are ready for public consumption. This work is no exception. Though my personal preference would have been to take much more time with this manuscript, the needs of the reader have been paramount in my mind. Convinced of the importance of this message I now release it, fully aware that a better book could have been written. I trust the reader will keep that in mind.

Books are not written in a vacuum. I am indebted to other writers who have also written much more exhaustively on this topic than I have. In this work I stand upon their shoulders. My overwhelming desire is that these words will bring glory to God and edify the Church of God as it strives to live out the true meaning of biblical faith in the world today. To God be the glory in the Church throughout the ages. Amen.

Truth Decay

Everywhere one turns today, the theme of passion for God can be heard throughout the Body of Christ. Books on developing spiritual passion continue to be among the most popular on the Christian market. Christian conferences on the theme are common fare throughout the land, usually drawing large numbers. Prayer conferences where people spend hours in worship and prayer have also gained in popularity over the last two decades. It seems that people are hungry to learn all they can about the passionate pursuit of God.

The growth in interest in this theme is certainly encouraging. Just as the return of appetite is often the first sign that a person has recovered from illness, in the same way a renewed appetite for God is evidence that many in the community of faith today have recovered from spiritual sickness. Previously, Christians may have soothed their consciences while doing little to create a deep appetite for God. Today, many are hungry to know God and pursue Him passionately. For all who love Him this is certainly cause for rejoicing.

Yet despite signs of increased passion for God in the Church, there is also reason for concern. Much of the spoken word, as well as literature on the subject of the passionate life, focuses largely on the pursuit of spiritual experiences as the primary way to increase passion for God. Precious little deals with the pursuit of *truth* as an important component of the passionate life. In fact, many popular devotional writers today totally ignore this aspect of the passionate life, even teaching that the pursuit of truth and the pursuit of God are in opposition and that believers must choose between them. In the preface of one of the most popular books on passion for God on the market today, the author draws a clear distinction between those that are ardently pursuing God and those content to "camp out around some "dusty old truth." By characterizing biblical truth this way ("dusty old truth") the author sets up an adversarial relationship between the pursuit of God on the one hand, and the pursuit of truth on the other. One might be tempted to excuse this as mere hyperbole, yet much later in the book the author refers to the New Testament letters as "old love letters" and urges his readers not to content themselves reading old correspondence but always and ever seek after fresh revelation.

If these were just the sentiments of a single writer we would not be concerned. Sadly though, many other spiritual writers today express similar sentiments regarding the place biblical truth should occupy in the pursuit of Christian spirituality. Whereas the Church once viewed intellectual conviction and belief in truth to be a major aspect of Christian spirituality, it seems this no longer is the case.

Why the reason for the change? In many ways these writers are reflecting the increasing 'anti-intellectual' and 'anti-truth' attitude in the culture today, including the religious culture. Christian statistician George Barna astutely observes,

> "The religious climate in America these days reflects the true soul of the population: one which thirsts for experience rather than knowledge, for exposure rather than understanding, for choices rather than the simplicity and the security of a limited set of alternatives."

While Barna is reflecting on the general religious climate as a whole, this trend can now be seen among many Evangelicals and Christians who hold to orthodox Christian teaching as well. A reticence to define themselves biblically now exists in many churches today. The general belief seems to be that by accepting the perimeters of Scripture they are (to borrow Barna's term) defining themselves by a "limited set of alternatives."

Nowhere is this trend more evident than among those believers who have traditionally laid greater stress on the need for the power of the Holy Spirit in the Church: *Pentecostals* and *Charismatics*. While they are not the only ones to stress the importance of a deeper work of the Spirit in the Church, they have certainly led the way in recapturing the teaching of the New Testament regarding the presence and power of the Spirit for normative Christian living and church life. Pentecostal and Charismatic churches are among the fastest growing worldwide today due in part to this important emphasis. Yet while Pentecostal/ Charismatic believers have led the way in recapturing this important biblical emphasis, they are often sorely lacking when it comes to the passionate pursuit of divine truth. Why are those claiming a deeper work of the Spirit often the shallowest biblically? There are many rea- sons, but the primary one is that many of these believers have been taught to be deeply suspicious of the *mind* when it comes to the pur- suit of Christian spirituality. For many Pentecostals and Charismatics, spirituality has become more about seeking after direct experiences with God than developing the mind to grasp biblical truth.

As a result of the denigration of the mind, many Pentecostal and Charismatic believers today have accepted the notion that they must choose between "living in the mind" or ignoring the mind and "liv- ing in the Spirit." Since these seem to be the only options, passionate spirituality wins out every time. After all, if the choices are between passionate spirituality versus intellectual development, who wouldn't choose passionate spirituality? Thankfully, such a dichotomy is no- where taught in Scripture. On the contrary, Scripture asserts that a Christian can (and must) develop his or her mind to the *fullest* without sacrificing in the least passionate spirituality. Indeed, as I will argue in this work, the development of the mind is an important component of the passionate life and therefore cannot be ignored.

One burden I have for this work is that it will help in furthering to reconcile the divide between Pentecostal/Charismatic believers and Evangelicals. Until fairly recently, each of these two groups have been deeply suspicious of the other. Pentecostal/Charismatic believers, who have traditionally laid greater stress on the person and work of the Holy Spirit, often view Evangelicals as void of the Spirit, lacking any real passion for God. Evangelicals, on the other hand, tend to perceive Pentecostal/Charismatic believers as biblically shallow and doctrinally unstable (a charge which is often justified). Yet, as believers increasingly abandon this false dichotomy between passionate spirituality on the one hand and strenuous thinking on the other, those in each camp are forced to reevaluate their position. Many Evangelicals, while not fully embracing all the nuances of Pentecostal/Charismatic theology, have come to understand that an emphasis on the power of the Spirit is both biblical and vital to church life. The result has been that many Evangelicals have begun seeking for more evidence of the Spirit's power in their own churches. At the same time many Charismatics, having grown tired of the superficiality of subjective experientialism, are hungering for a spirituality that is rooted in solid biblical scholarship and theology.

One evidence of this new attitude is the popularity of the ministry of John Piper, pastor of Bethlehem Baptist Church in Minneapolis, Minnesota. He is an Evangelical whose passionate preaching and gifted writings has been warmly embraced by both Evangelicals and Charismatics. Dr. Piper has exposed many in this generation to the teachings of American pastor and theologian Jonathan Edwards, a man who himself drank deeply from both streams. Edwards was certainly no slouch when it came to intellectual development; in fact, many believe he possessed the finest mind America ever produced. Yet Edwards was anything but a cold, sterile theologian. His journals abound with accounts of his deep spiritual experiences as he partook of the First Great Awakening in colonial New England. Edwards normalized the idea that one could think deeply without sacrificing spiritual experience. The writings of Edwards, as mediated through John Piper, have contributed greatly to helping people realize that one does not have to choose between *truth* and *power* in the quest for a passionate Christianity.

Other modern writers in the Edwards' tradition have also emphasized this vital theme, such as Doug Bannister in his work *The Word and Power Church*, Sam Storms in *Convergence: Spiritual Journeys of a Charismatic Calvinist*, and Rick Nanez in his excellent work, *Full Gospel, Fractured Minds*. These works vividly demonstrate how these two emphases should work together, and they have contributed greatly to the emergence of churches where both the pursuit of God and the pursuit of truth are held in proper balance. Recent years have even seen the emergence of entire church networks where the passionate pursuit of truth and rich experience of the power of the Spirit are both pursued.

In many ways this work reflects my own journey as one who has richly drawn from both camps. My spiritual roots are in the Pentecostal/Charismatic tradition where an immediate experience of God through the power of the Holy Spirit is both taught and experienced. I am grateful for my personal spiritual history in this camp, and am firmly convinced that this emphasis on the power of the Spirit in the Church today is not only biblical, but vital to recapturing normative church life. We ignore it at our own peril, as the Church through the ages has often discovered.

Yet, while the totality of my church experience has been in Charismatic churches, I have also learned much from Evangelicals. From them, I have learned the importance of having a biblically informed faith. In fact, I credit Evangelical writers with keeping me from total boredom in my Christian life! Early on in my spiritual sojourn I found myself bored (intellectually) with what my local church had to offer and began to seek for intellectual stimulation in my Christian life (not intellectualism, but an understanding of the truth to satisfy my mind as well as my heart). It was then that I was introduced to the writings of men such as J.I Packer, C.S. Lewis, and Charles Spurgeon who stimulated me to think deeply to the glory of God. Through their writings, I learned the simple but powerful truth; that the pathway to passion for God is ever and always through the *mind*.

Having drunk deeply now from both streams for over thirty years, I have never felt as if I had to choose between them. As a Charismatic (in terms of belief in the immediacy of the power of the Holy Spirit in the Church) I continue to feel at home among those churches which seek for a richer experience of God's Spirit and power. As an Evangelical (theologically) I am quite comfortable exercising my mind to the fullest in pursuit of understanding divine truth. In some ways this has made me an enigma to both camps (add to this the fact that I'm Jewish and people really get confused). Standing in line to board a plane in South America one day, I struck up a conversation with an Evangelical missionary returning to the States on furlough. Before long, we were deeply engaged in a theological discussion. Since I was fully acquainted with the contours of his theology, I was able to converse with him on the subject with relative ease. All was well until he discovered that I was a Charismatic, at which point he became visibly shaken. He confessed that he had never encountered such a thing as a "thinking" Charismatic and seemed totally bewildered by my existence.

Yet some Charismatics have had difficulty understanding me as well. I once recommended a book by an Evangelical scholar in a church network newsletter, and took some flack for it from fellow Charismatics who were puzzled by my willingness to recommend a book written by someone who was not "Spirit-filled." There was no consideration as to whether the author's ideas were biblical or not; since he was not Pentecostal or Charismatic, they (wrongly) concluded they could learn nothing from his book.

Why I Wrote This Book

In many ways this work reflects my own journey from the superficiality of Charismatic church life to a more mature, biblical faith.

Along with many Charismatics today, I have grown tired of the shallowness and superficiality of a faith rooted chiefly in experience rather than one properly informed by Scripture. As I stated earlier, I have no desire to deny the richness of the power and life of the Spirit which I have known; I simply long for a faith that not only brings with it valid spiritual experience, but satisfies intellectually as well.

How do we find such a faith? Sadly, for Charismatic and Pentecostal believers today there is precious little that has been written to guide them in this quest. That is my hope for this present work. I want it to serve as a guide for believers who know the power of the Spirit but need encouragement to pursue a biblically informed faith as well. Yet the reader should beware if he or she expects to find here a sort of 'how-to' manual—"seven steps for creating passion for truth" and the like. I avoid this approach precisely because I do not believe there is a simple formula for producing passion for truth in the Church. Rather, my intent in this work is to uncover the basic biblical realities underlying both the creation and maintenance of spiritual passion. I am persuaded that it is the ignorance of these things which accounts for the waning of passion for truth we see in the Church today.

If I were to summarize this book, I would say that it deals largely with the nature of biblical authority and its application to believers in the context of Christian discipleship. Great harm has resulted from the practice of encouraging people to actively seek after spiritual experiences without a corresponding emphasis on the need to submit to the authority of Scripture. My purpose is to practically illustrate why the authority of Scripture is so critical to healthy Christian living. In seeking to set forth the importance of biblical authority in the Church though, I am in no way promoting an "experience-less" Christianity. I am aware that many advocates of the restoration of Bible-authority in the Church often promote a faith which is little more than a 'rational belief in propositions.' In my mind, that is as unscriptural as a faith rooted *solely* in experience. What I commend here is that believers and churches seek after *all* the Scripture teaches as being normative for spiritual experience, while fully submitting themselves to the authority of Scripture.

To accomplish this, I have divided the material in this book into three sections each of which highlights some aspect of the loss of passion for truth in the Church today and what is needed for its full restoration. Section one, *The Tragic Loss of Truth,* focuses on three trends which have contributed greatly to the loss of passion for truth in the Church— the overt *subjectivity* in the modern Church, popular notions regarding *revival,* and the rise of Christian *Pragmatism.* Chapter One, *'Are You Experienced?'* examines the danger of a faith rooted solely in subjective experience without the safeguards of the authority of Scripture. Chapter Two, *'Blowin' in the Wind,'* looks at popular ideas regarding revival and how they have contributed to the diminishing of the passionate pursuit of of truth among believers. The final chapter in that section is entitled *'The Virtue of Unoriginality'* and challenges popular notions of how the Church should respond to Postmodernism.

Section Two, *'A Mindless Faith,'* focuses on the place God has deemed that the mind should have in the Christian life. I am convinced that it is the unscriptural notions regarding the intellect in the pursuit of Christian spirituality which account for much of the loss of passion for truth in the Church today. Since the passionate pursuit of truth requires the fullest use of the mind, recovering a biblical understanding of the mind is crucial to the restoration of passion. Four chapters in this section will deal with this. Chapter Four, *'A Mind is a Terrible Thing to Waste,'* focuses on the central place God intended the mind to have in the creation of human beings. Chapter Five, *'Transformed by the Removing of Your Mind',* reviews some of the current notions regarding the intellect in three key areas of Christian living: *faith, guidance,* and *evangelism.* Chapter Six, *'The Cure for Boredom with God,'* examines the place *theology* holds in safeguarding the mind from boredom. Finally, Chapter Seven, *'Enjoying God Without Losing Your Mind,'* dispels the myth that the active use of the mind lessens the enjoyment of the emotions in the Christian life. It introduces the reader to the lives of Jonathan Edwards and the English Puritans—shining examples of those who developed their minds to the fullest without losing passion for God Himself.

Section Three, '*Restoring* a *Passion for Truth,*' examines those things God has given the Church for the nurturing of passion for truth. While written largely with leaders in mind, everyone will find some helpful recommendations in this section. Chapter Eight, '*That Dirty Word Doctrine,*' makes the case that teaching doctrine is an important part of creating passion for truth in the house of God. Chapter Nine, '*Is There a Preacher in the House?*' reminds us that preaching is still God's ordained means of fueling passion for truth in the Church. And finally Chapter Ten, '*Truth is a Person,*' examines the relationship between the written Word (Scripture) and the Incarnate Word (Christ). It reminds us that truth is infinitely more than mere belief in propositions, but a living *Person*—Jesus Christ, who is the flesh and blood embodiment of truth.

My earnest desire is that these words are not only a source of great encouragement but are used by the Master to produce a harvest of passion for truth in those who love Him with a pure heart. To God be the glory!

THE TRAGIC LOSS
OF TRUTH

CHAPTER ONE

Are You Experienced?

While living in South Florida in 1971 I had a life-transforming encounter with Jesus Christ, altering the entire direction of my life. As a young, disillusioned Jew desperately searching for answers to the deepest questions of life, I least expected to find them in the Gospel of Jesus Christ. After God transformed my older brother setting him free from drug addiction through the power of the Gospel, I began finding myself being strangely drawn to my Messiah, Jesus of Nazareth. One autumn evening while attending a Gospel meeting at my brother's behest, I experienced the life transforming power of the Gospel and passed from death to life. In a word, I became a "new creature in Christ" (II Corinthians 5:17).

Immediately after my conversion, I entered my first experience of church life in a small church in Miami Beach, Florida which my brother had helped start. Eager to learn all I could about my newfound faith, I immersed myself totally in the life of the church, faithfully attending all of the church services and participating in all of the church's weekly activities. Worshipping with the Lord's people and listening to my pastor's fiery messages calling us to a deeper commitment to God shaped my early Christian life. At the conclusion of each service, I responded to the invitation to recommit my life once again to God and his service. It was during those days I first sensed a call to the ministry, and began preparing myself for my life's work of teaching the Word of God.

Whatever plans I had though, they were rudely interrupted in 1973 when a leader in our church announced he had received a (supposed) revelation from God that the *rapture* of the Church (the secret return of Jesus Christ before his Second Coming) would occur before the end of that year. At the time he shared it with us (myself and a few friends) we had, what seemed at the time, a powerful experience of the presence of God which we subsequently interpreted as confirmation of the revelation. Other experiences of God's presence soon followed. All of these experiences served to strengthen our faith in the revelation. We were thoroughly persuaded that some time in the next few months, the Lord would return and take us to our celestial home.

Besides trying to persuade a few other friends, we set our focus entirely on the coming of the Lord to take us out of this world. Yet, if that initial revelation rocked my world, it was soon rocked again when my older brother called one morning to inform me that the word we had received was not from God! Needless to say, I was devastated when I heard it. A flood of questions filled my mind: "How could I have been so deceived? Hadn't I received many indications from the Spirit that it was true?" In the months that followed I desperately sought answers to these questions as I struggled to come to terms with what happened.

At first answers were slow in coming. Yet as I continued to pray and examine the Scriptures, I began to understand why I had been so easily deceived. The most obvious thing was that I had failed to examine the word in the light of what was written (Holy Scripture). If I had submitted it to the scrutiny of Scripture I would have immediately known that the so-called revelation was contrary to what was written, and therefore was to be rejected. I determined in the future that I would examine all my experiences in the light of Holy Scripture so as to never be deceived again.

Yet, besides failing to examine the word in the light of the Scripture, I also realized that I had profoundly *misinterpreted* the meaning of my own experiences. I had mistaken a heightened awareness of God's presence as a confirmation of the revelation. I learned from this that I should never to be to quick in assigning meaning to an experience without having adequate time to assess it. Along with the importance of prayerfully examining all experiences in the light of the Word, I realized the importance of submitting my experiences to the scrutiny of mature Christians as well. I came out of this season with a new determination to study the Scriptures so as to never be deceived again. Many of the disciplines I developed during those days have been with me now for over thirty years.

Objective and Subjective Realms

Looking back on this experience I realized how God used it in my life to teach me many important things. But perhaps the most important lesson I learned was the importance of distinguishing between the two realms which God is at work in in the life of every believer. They are the *objective* and *subjective* realms. Failure to recognize the difference between these two realms can have devastating results. Let me explain.

All genuine experience with God lies in the *subjective* realm, where God works in the inner life of the believer. These may include a heightened sense of God's presence during worship or joyous emotions in the service of God. For each believer these experiences will vary. Yet God intends for each of us to enjoy a rich array of spiritual experiences in the subjective realm. In fact, that is why He has given us His Spirit to reside in our hearts in the first place; to make known to each of us the reality of the historical Christ so that we might experience Him in a deep and personal way.

Yet while God planned for us to enjoy a rich array of experiences in the subjective realm, He never intended for us to be *governed* by that realm. Rather, we are to be governed by the *objective* realm of divine truth. What do I mean by the objective realm of divine truth? The dictionary defines *objective* as "not being influenced by personal feelings or opinions in considering or representing facts." To be objective is to represent facts as they are, not allowing personal feelings or preferences to influence us. So living by the objective realm of divine truth simply means that we are living under the authority of Holy Scripture instead of our personal feelings or preferences.

The cultivation of Christian spirituality therefore requires that we focus on both of these realms. To ignore either is to distort the meaning of the Christian life and ensure a fragmented Christian experience. Yet, throughout the worldwide body of Christ today, we see many believers who emphasize one to the exclusion of the other. For example, some believers focus on cultivating spiritual experiences while ignoring entirely the objective realm of divine truth. For them, the spiritual person is the one who collects the most spiritual experiences. This has produced a generation of believers who give lip service to the authority of Scripture, but are in reality governed by the subjective realm.

As a young believer I once heard the popular saying, "A man with an experience is never at the mercy of a man with an argument." I remember being greatly impressed by that statement when I first heard it. It seemed likely to me that a person with an experience could not be easily talked out of it. Yet after my experience in my first church, I began to question the validity of that statement. I knew it was possible to have an experience which I thought I understood, only to discover I had "misunderstood profoundly" as I once heard Dr. R.C. Sproul say! On the other hand, a rational and reasonable argument based on objective truth is true regardless of one's personal experience of it.

In reaction to this emphasis on the subjective, other believers have made our need to be governed by the objective realm their primary focus. Yet in so doing they tend to play down the validity of spiritual experiences altogether. For them, the Christian life is little more than studying and believing Bible propositions. This is also wrong. A faith which denies *valid* spiritual experiences is as unscriptural as one totally rooted in spiritual experiences. While God never intended that we be governed by the subjective realm, He has purposed that we enjoy a rich array of experiences.

That God intends for human beings to live in both realms is evident by the fact that when Adam and Eve were first created and placed in the Garden of Eden, they richly enjoyed both. We know, for example, that they were invited each day to have fellowship with the Lord God in the cool of the day (Genesis 3:8). It is not hard to imagine how they must have experienced a rich array of emotions as they encountered the divine presence in the Garden. Yet they were not to be ruled by this realm, evidenced by the fact that the Lord God tied the exercise of their rule over the planet, to obedience to His objective word. It was *objective* in that it came to them from *without*, having been first spoken to them by God Himself. Apart from such communication they would have never known God's will regarding the two trees in the Garden.

That they understood this word is evident from the fact that when the serpent began his campaign against the woman, she was able to clearly recite God's word to him (though adding her own interpretation to it). That word contained both a gracious provision ("you may eat freely of all the trees of the Garden") as well as a clear prohibition ("you shall not eat of the tree of knowledge of good and evil").

It is important to note that when Satan mounted his assault against the woman, he did so by first impugning the integrity of God's Word. His goal was to raise doubts regarding what He had said so that she would think that she could now disobey without impunity (Genesis 3:1). And it worked. As she listened to the serpent she looked at the tree, no longer from the perspective of God's word, but through her own subjective lens: "When the woman saw that the fruit of the tree was good for food and pleasing to the *eye*, and also *desirable* for gaining wisdom, she took some and ate it" (Genesis 3:6). Instead of containing forbidden fruit, the tree now seemed to offer her a *better* way of fulfilling her God-given destiny. She ate, and gave some to her husband. And the rest, as they say, is history.

A Crisis of Authority

This account of the temptation of Eve in the Garden provides us with a perfect job description of the enemy. His *modus operandi* has changed little in thousands of years— why should it when it has worked so well for so long? He always seeks to distort the Word of God so that human beings will treat it with contempt and subsequently disobey it.

What the Serpent did in the Garden was tempt Eve to transfer God's authority from the objective realm of divine authority through the word, to the subjective realm. Eve faced a real 'crisis of authority' in the Garden: Would she choose to live under the authority of God's objective word, or else allow her own subjectivity to determine how she would live? She clearly chose the latter and the entire human race was plunged into darkness. Though not as momentous as the crisis Eve faced in the Garden, this same crisis of authority faces God's people in every generation. The difference is that Adam and Eve heard the word spoken in the Garden, while the word comes to us as a written revelation. Nevertheless, it is still the authoritative word by which God intends for us to be governed.

We should expect, therefore, that just as Satan tempted Eve to reject God's spoken word in the Garden, so he will also tempt us to reject his written Word. Judging from what we observe in the Church today it would seem he has been quite successful! Our churches are filled with people who seek after spiritual experiences, yet have very little desire to know God's *objective* word in Scripture. Whenever we are willing to give more attention to the subjective realm of experience than the objective realm of divine truth we succumb to the same temptation as Eve.

I once heard (via cassette) a pastor in Philadelphia named Dave Harvey preach a message which addressed this 'crisis of authority' in the Church today. The title of the message was the "Subjective Captivity of the Church" and was drawn from the title of one of Martin Luther's tracts which he wrote soon after discovering God's justifying grace. The real title of Luther's tract was the "Babylonian Captivity of the Church." It was a scathing indictment of the Catholic Church in his day which Luther likened to ancient Babylon in the Old Testament and their enslavement of the people of Judah. For Luther, the Reformation was God's call to free his people from bondage in the same way God freed Judah from slavery to Babylon.

In his message Pastor Harvey asked the question, "If Luther were alive today to view the Western Church what title would he give to the tract describing it?" His conclusion was that he would probably call it the '*Subjective* Captivity of the Church' rather than the 'Babylonian Captivity of the Church.' Pastor Harvey suggested that Luther would call it this in order to draw attention to the fact that many believers today have become slaves to the subjective realm. Here is how Pastor Harvey defined the Subjective Captivity of the Church: "the encroaching tendency today to exalt feelings, emotions, impressions, and experiences above the Word of God." I heartily agree with this definition. Whenever people allow inward impressions, experiences, emotions and other things to have more influence in their lives than Scripture, they become slaves to the subjective. The end result is that the authority of Scripture is seriously undermined.

Pastor Harvey's comparison between Luther's tract and the modern Church is an important one. In Luther's day the Church abrogated to itself the ultimate authority for determining how the faithful should live. Luther and the Reformers coined the phrase *Sola Scriptura* (Scripture alone) to underscore their belief that the written Word of God alone was the ultimate authority for the life and practice of the people of God. People often think the Reformation was primarily about the restoration of long forgotten biblical doctrines such as 'justification by faith' and the 'priesthood of all believers.' While it is true that the Reformation restored these vital doctrines, at its core was a restoration of biblical *authority* itself. Luther and the Reformers opposed the Church when she claimed for herself an authority greater than that of Scripture. For them, God's Word was the final authority for life and godliness.

The crisis of authority facing the Church in our day is every bit as real as the one Luther faced in his days, yet it is not so much about the Church abrogating to itself the ultimate authority over God's people, but subjective experience. When believers allow their own experiences to have more authority in their lives than God's Word, it is clearly a manifestation of the 'Subjective Captivity of the Church.' This came home to me several years ago while attending one of the small group meetings of our local church in a home near where I lived. Before the meeting began I was seated next to a woman whom I knew fairly well. She began sharing with me a particular struggle she was having at the time. After describing her struggle, I began making a few observations from Scripture which I thought applied to her situation. She listened politely at first, but the longer I spoke, the more annoyed she became. Finally she interrupted me saying, "I appreciate what you are telling me, but that is something for my head; what I need right now is something for my heart!"

I was totally amazed at her response. Here was a Christian woman who dismissed entirely what Scripture had to say to her perceiving it as something for her "head and not for her heart." In the final analysis, the Word of God had little real authority in her life. While it might provide her with some useful information or inspiration, it had little to offer when it came to determining how she should live.

Unfortunately, the attitude that woman expressed towards Scripture that day is not at all uncommon in the Church today. Few believers allow the Word of God to really govern their lives. One evidence of that is the fact that there is very little Bible instruction in many churches today. A number of years ago I spent an entire day with a group of pastors who had come to together to discuss the reasons for the biblical illiteracy of their members. The day was spent discussing ways in which hunger for God's Word might again be cultivated in our churches. The common consensus was that unless people began to hunger again for God's Word, the health of the churches would be in serious jeopardy.

I repeat: the Church faces a 'crisis of authority' today every bit as real as Luther faced in his day. The only remedy is for us to return to the full authority of Scripture just as Luther and the Reformers did. This alone will curb the rising tide of subjectivism which characterizes much of Western Christianity today. Returning to the full authority of

Scripture means more than merely using the Bible in our sermons or church liturgy, but building lives solidly on the full authority of God's Word written.

The Reformation was precipitated by the question, "Is Scripture, or is human dogma and tradition the ultimate authority for what Christians believe and practice?" Luther and the Reformers answered unhesitatingly that ultimate authority must reside in Holy Scripture alone. In every age the Church has had to answer this question. What will we be our answer in our day?

The Sufficiency of Scripture

During his earthly ministry, Jesus told a story in which he warned of the inevitable judgment awaiting those who trust in riches rather than God. That story known as 'The Rich Man and Lazarus' is recorded in Luke's Gospel (Luke 16:19-31). While its original purpose was to address the dangers of covetousness, it also has something important to say regarding the full authority of God's Word. I quote it here in its entirety:

> "There was a rich man who was dressed in purple and fine linen and lived in luxury every day. At his gate was laid a beggar named Lazarus, covered with sores and longing to eat what fell from the rich man's table. Even the dogs came and licked his sores.
>
> "The time came when the beggar died and the angels carried him to Abraham's side. The rich man also died and was buried. In hell, where he was in torment, he looked up and saw Abraham far away, with Lazarus by his side.
>
> * So he called to him, 'Father Abraham, have pity on me and send Lazarus to dip the tip of his finger in water and cool my tongue, because I am in agony in this fire.'
>
> "But Abraham replied, 'Son, remember that in your lifetime you received your good things, while Lazarus received bad things, but now he is comforted here and you are in agony. And besides all this, between us and you a great chasm has been fixed, so that those who want to go from here to you cannot, nor can anyone cross over from there to us.'

> *"He answered, 'Then I beg you, father, send Lazarus to my father's house, for I have five brothers. Let him warn them, so that they will not also come to this place of torment.'*
>
> *"Abraham replied, 'They have Moses and the Prophets; let them listen to them.'*
>
> *'No, father Abraham,' he said, 'but if someone from the dead goes to them, they will repent.'*
>
> *"He said to him, 'If they do not listen to Moses and the Prophets, they will not be convinced even if someone rises from the dead.'"*

Lazarus and the rich man lived very different lives on earth and had very different rewards awaiting them in eternity. Lazarus was carried by the angels into the bosom of Abraham to live in eternal bliss, while the rich man descended into the terrors of hell. Tormented in flames, the rich man appealed to father Abraham to "allow Lazarus to dip the tip of his finger in water and cool my tongue because I am in agony in this fire" (16:24). Abraham denied this request reminding him that, while he lived a life of luxury on earth enjoying "good things," Lazarus had received the bad. Besides (he told him) a great chasm was fixed between them, making movement between the two realms impossible (16:26).

With the possibility of receiving comfort for himself gone, the rich man turned his attention towards getting help for his family members: "Send Lazarus to my father's house so that they will not also come to this place of torment" (16:27). Abraham denied this request as well reminding him that his family members were already sufficiently warned since they had "Moses and the Prophets" (16:29). Nevertheless, the rich man continued his appeal, convinced that if his brothers saw someone rise from the dead, they would believe (16:30). Yet father Abraham assured him that would not be the case. If they did not already believe what was written, no supernatural sign would convince them: "If they do not listen to Moses and the Prophets they will not be convinced even if someone rises from the dead" (16:31).

In his rebuke to the rich man, Father Abraham alludes to an important aspect of the nature of Scripture that theologians commonly refer to as the sufficiency of Scripture. It means that Scripture is utterly *sufficient* to provide us with all we will ever need to know concerning the divine will. That the rich man had a faulty view of Scripture is evident by the request he made to Abraham to send Lazarus to his brothers in the hope that, if they saw someone rise from the dead, they might believe. He did not believe that the Scriptures were sufficient to warn them. If he did, he would not have asked Abraham to send someone from the dead to warn them.

Some believers today resemble the rich man in that they believe unless people see signs and wonders they will not be persuaded. Years ago, there saw the emergence of the so-called "Signs and Wonders Movement" which focused on producing evidences of power when the Gospel is preached, so that people would be induced to believe. This movement was not entirely wrong; after all, Jesus did promise signs and wonders as confirmation of the preached word (Mark 16:17). Yet, we must always remember that these signs were given to *confirm* the word, never replace it. The belief that signs and wonders alone will convince an unbelieving world is a gross caricature of Scripture, and seriously downplays the sufficiency of God's written word.

This doctrine of the sufficiency of Scripture does not suggest that that the Bible answers every question we might have on any topic. There are many things we might wish to know which Scripture simply doesn't address. What it does mean, though, is that when it comes to providing us with a revelation of God leading to salvation and instruction in godly living, Scripture is totally sufficient (II Timothy 3:16-17). Wayne Grudem helps us to understand this important aspect of Scripture:

> "The sufficiency of Scripture means that Scripture contained all the words of God He intended his people to have at each stage of redemptive history, and that it now contains all the words of God we need for salvation, for trusting him perfectly, and for obeying him perfectly" (*Systematic Theology*, Wayne Grudem, page 127)

The phrase *Sola Scriptura* (Scripture alone) coined during the Reformation conveyed a similar idea. By *sola* (alone), the Reformers did not mean only Scripture alone should be read, since they themselves produced many other writings. Rather, they meant that the Bible *alone* contained all that human beings would ever need for cultivating the knowledge of God, of themselves, and of God's will for how to live. This belief in the sufficiency of Scripture was at the core of their dissent with the Catholic Church. Since Scripture alone addressed all matters of human salvation, it must be the authoritative guide for the children of God. That meant that if the edicts of popes and Church councils contradicted Scripture (as it often did), the children of God must obey what is written rather than human traditions and religious decrees.

Did the Reformers worry that by placing so much emphasis on the authority of Scripture they ran the risk of minimizing the place spiritual experience holds in our lives? Not at all. They knew that holding firmly to the truth of Holy Scripture would not jeopardize one iota their enjoyment of spiritual experiences. Church history bears this out. It is replete with examples of men and women of rich spiritual experience who held firmly to the full authority of Scripture. In the final section of this book I highlight the life of Jonathan Edwards; a man who held tenaciously to the full authority of Scripture, yet enjoyed a rich array of spiritual experiences.

Summing It Up

I recently had the pleasure of attending the opening of a unique museum of the Bible which came to our city. The museum contained several original manuscripts of Scripture, including a rare glimpse at various Dead Sea scroll fragments. It was arranged in such a way as that the oldest manuscripts were on display first, as you entered, followed by those which came later. Thus arranged, it allowed the viewer to easily grasp the development of the Bible from ancient text to its present form in the various English translations we now have. It was a powerful reminder, that from its inception, God Himself has been actively working to preserve his written Word. I left with a new appreciation of the preciousness of Scripture.

Today, it is critical that believers rediscover the full authority of Scripture without minimizing the richness of spiritual experience in the least. The truth is, both (spiritual experience and knowledge of Scripture) belong to us. Both are our spiritual heritage. Yet it is only as we live under the full authority of Scripture, that we can safely pursue the experiential Christian life without becoming slaves to the subjective realm.

May God hasten the day when *Sola Scriptura* is once again heard throughout the land.

Chapter Two

Blowin' in the Wind

In the mid 1970's, I moved to a small town in Western North Carolina, to assist a friend in the establishing of a new church plant. Before moving, I was still living in South Florida, pastoring the church I had joined after my conversion. Sensing that I could not take that church any further, I accepted the invitation to help my friend establish this new church. The prospect of this new work excited me, and I looked forward to the challenge of seeing a new local church planted from the ground up.

Before leaving Florida though, I had several conversations with friends who were engaged in the study of the history of revival. As I listened to them describe these mighty times when God poured out His Spirit upon his Church, I had a great desire to acquaint myself with the history of these mighty moves of God. So I began to read everything I could get my hands on the subject of revival. Before long, I learned about such mighty moves of God as the *First* and *Second Great Awakenings*, those twin outpourings of God's Spirit which shaped the founding of our own country, as well as mightily impacting England. I also read about the Welsh Revival of the early twentieth century which shook the nation of Wales.

I was especially fascinated with what I had read about the ministry of American revivalist Charles Finney, who lived in upstate New

York and ministered in the late nineteenth century. According to his biographer, wherever Finney went revival broke out, resulting in the conversion of thousands of people. Unlike other revivalists before him, Finney used unique methods to promote his revivals. He did not believe that revival was a miracle at all, but the result of the application of certain means. According to Finney, in the same way a farmer plants seed in the ground with the full expectation of a harvest, so preachers who faithfully plant the seed of the Gospel in hearts could expect revival to follow. The accounts of his success throughout upstate New York seemed to confirm his theology. Today, Finney's views on revival dominate much of the Church's thinking on the subject.

The more I studied these mighty moves of God, the more convinced I was that God was sending me to North Carolina to promote a powerful revival in the region. When I arrived I began implementing everything I had learned from the books I had read. Knowing that prayer was a key component in the initiation of any revival, I prayed fervently that God would pour out revival fire on Western North Carolina. I rose early each morning pleading with God to pour out his Spirit upon our church and spent many days in fasting and prayer as well. I was thoroughly convinced that if I faithfully kept up this vigil, the entire region would soon be engulfed in revival flames.

I had also learned from my studies that brokenness was a key component of revival. One particular book I read highlighted the life and ministry of Evan Roberts, the young man God had used to spawn the Welsh Revival. Roberts taught that only after a person was sufficiently broken (deeply convicted of sin) could he be a vessel fit for God to use to bring revival. I began longing that God would break me so that I might be worthy of being a vessel for revival. I began carefully examining myself before God, confessing to him any sins I had committed (including sins I had not committed). I was sure that before long God would sufficiently break me so that I could be an instrument fitting to bring revival.

After several months of keeping up this vigil I began feeling the first pangs of weariness. Secretly, I wondered if I would be able to keep it up until the power fell. Despite my weariness, I pressed on. I was thoroughly convinced that my hard work would eventually be rewarded, and the fires of revival would burn in our region.

Yet despite my efforts revival never did come (as far as I know it still hasn't). Within a few months I actually left the area and moved to Detroit, Michigan where I served on the pastoral staff of an inner city church. Though I was occupied in my new role in this church, I was desperate for answers as to why I had failed to see revival come to North Carolina. My first reaction was to blame myself for failing to meet the necessary conditions. Perhaps if I had spent more time in prayer or allowed God to break me more thoroughly, I would have achieved the desired results.

Yet, once I moved beyond feeling responsible, I turned to Scripture to see if I could find any answers as to why I had failed to see revival come. The first thing that struck me was how little the subject of revival even comes up in God's Word. From my study of the history of revival, I had come to believe that they were God's major means of changing both the Church and the world. Yet apart from a few scant verses here and there, the Bible had very little to say about it. I found this strange. If revival was God's main means of changing history, why didn't Scripture have more to say about it?

It was then that I discovered that God had a far more powerful and reliable provision for his people than revival. This realization would change my entire approach to ministry forever.

Revival Sometimes, the Gospel Always

Despite the fact that Scripture has little to say about it, much of the Christian Church today remains fascinated with the subject of revival. As I write, a new outpouring of revival is purported to be occurring in a southern state. Books, as well as spoken messages on the subject, continue to be widely distributed throughout much of the Body of Christ. This interest in revival is fueled in part by the belief that we are on the precipice of a worldwide outpouring of God's Spirit:

> "Another wave of God's presence is about to hit the shore of the church and the nations. It has happened before in differing times and seasons. I've carefully studied the history of revival in America and around the world, but another wave is coming that is going to be different—if we cooperate" (Tommy Tenney, *The God Chasers*, Thomas Nelson, page 49-50)

Why does the subject of revival remain so popular in the Church today? One of the reasons is the belief that *only* revival can fix what is wrong with the Church and bring needed change to our world. Many Christians today are fully persuaded that unless God pours out His Spirit as He has in the past, there is little reason to be hopeful.

Again, I am somewhat sympathetic to this view. After all, when God has poured out his Spirit on the Church in the past, it certainly brought massive change both to the Church and the society as a whole. So I am not surprised that people would long for God to move again in this fashion. This view (that the only hope for the Church is for God to pour out His Spirit as He did in times past) reminds me of the chorus from a popular song from the sixties written by one of my favorite theologians, Bob Dylan. The lyrics went like this:

> "The answer my friend is blowin' in the wind
> The answer is blowin' in the wind..."

Many subscribe to the theology of Dylan when it comes to revival. They believe that the answer for whatever ails in the Church is always "blowin' in the wind." Revival and the hope that it might come has become the default mode for many believers today. When things look really dim in the Church, they automatically fall back on the hope that revival will come and change everything.

As I stated before, my own study of the history of revival led me to embrace the theology of Dylan as well. Yet, after my failure to see revival come in North Carolina and my subsequent search of the Scriptures, I discovered that God's Word never presents revival as a sort of cure-all for the Church's ills. It simply is not there. While I certainly believe that Scripture *allows* for revival, it never presents it as the *ultimate* answer for the Church. I would say that it is *an* answer, but not necessarily *the* answer.

Incidentally, one of the reasons I don't believe revival is the ultimate answer for what ails the Church, is that we can never say with assurance when it will come. It is bound up with the sovereignty of God. We are certainly bidden to pray for it, yet since we can never know for sure when it will come, it stands to reason that it cannot be God's ultimate provision for the Church. This is because God has not pinned the welfare of his Church on what *might* happen in the future.

So if revival is not God's ultimate provision for his people at all times, what is? A pastor friend of mine in Indiana, Steve Chupp, once preached a sermon which I think best answers that question. That sermon entitled "Revival Sometimes, the Gospel Always" dealt with the relationship between revival and the Gospel. In the message, Pastor Chupp reminded his congregation that revival is a biblical phenomena that God, at various times throughout church history, has been pleased to send upon his Church. That being the case, he encouraged his congregation to pray that God would send revival upon them.

Yet then he played devil's advocate and asked his congregation, "What if God doesn't send revival when we ask for it?" His purpose was not to cast doubt upon their prayers but draw attention to the fact that God is not obligated to send revival whenever we ask for it. The remainder of the sermon focused on the fact that God has given his people a much greater provision than the fleeting promise of revival. *That provision is the Gospel.* It is the Gospel, rather than revival, that is God's ultimate provision for everything the Church will ever need. God has nothing else to offer other than what He has already given to the Church—the good news of Jesus Christ. In the remainder of the message Pastor Chupp talked about the power of the Gospel as God's ultimate provision for his people.

I agree wholeheartedly with Pastor Chupp. The Church never has to wait for something that *might* happen in the future since she already has the Gospel. If revival comes, she can rejoice, but if not, it doesn't matter for in the Gospel she has all things. I once expressed this confidence in the Gospel in a song I wrote for my first album. The first line went like this:

> "In the Gospel, I have found all that I need,
> In the Gospel, if I only would believe
> Mercy flowing down upon me,
> Oceans of his love..."

This confidence in the Gospel was stated even more clearly in the chorus:

> "I can't believe that the Gospel is free,
> I can't believe what it started in me
> If I had ten thousand years to proclaim
> The Gospel, praise his name!"

I am totally convinced that it is loss of confidence in the Gospel which accounts for much of the obsession with revival in the Church today. When we don't understand how God intends to meet all of our needs through the Gospel, we inevitably place our hope in something else; something we have not *yet* received. We latch on to these things precisely because we have lost confidence in the Gospel's power. Our greatest need therefore is to come to a more complete understanding and appreciation of the truth of the Gospel of God.

Perhaps the reader might ask at this juncture, "Hasn't the Church had the Gospel for two thousand years, while little has changed?" But is the assumption that the Church "has always had the Gospel" true? I don't think so. Examining what passes for the Gospel in many churches today, one could argue that much of what is called *Gospel* is actually a hodgepodge of the Gospel mixed with human tradition, legalism, and other elements. Many in our churches today remain strangers to the biblical Gospel altogether. In 1983, on the floor of a Christian convention, the attendees were asked a series of questions regarding their Christian faith including the question, "What is the Gospel." Of the many who attended, only one came close to giving a biblical answer. I don't think that means that they weren't true believers. It really reflects the poor job we have done in discipling people in the biblical Gospel.

Why are so many in the Church today strangers to the biblical Gospel? One reason is that they continue to operate on the belief that the Gospel gets us into the kingdom; then, after we are in, we need other things (discipleship, holiness, prayer, service, etc.) to keep us. So we effectively put the Gospel on the shelf, while we pursue these other things for our growth in the kingdom. Now there is nothing wrong with pursuing these things. Yet because we have put the Gospel on the shelf we pursue them in an atmosphere other than the Gospel. And they become burdensome having not been sweetened by the grace of God in the Gospel. Trying to live the Christian life apart from the grace of God which comes through the Gospel is an exercise in futility.

In the first century, the apostles built churches solidly upon the Gospel they had received. For them, the Gospel was not merely the message by which people entered the kingdom, but the message which guaranteed their full maturity in Christ as well. This came home to me powerfully several years ago when I began seriously studying the letters of Paul in the New Testament. There is no doubt that Paul's success as an apostle was due to his confidence in the Gospel. For Paul, the Gospel was both the message by which sinners were saved as well as that which guaranteed their continued growth in Christ. Paul didn't have two messages—one for the unsaved and one for the saved—but a Gospel by which the lost were saved and through which believers achieved full maturity in Christ as well.

What I realized as I began studying his letters was that many of the churches Paul wrote to were having problems precisely because they had departed from his Gospel.   For example, Paul wrote a letter to the church at Colosse (Colossians), a church actually started by one of his associates. The believers there had allowed a form of Gnostic mysticism which seduced them from the purity of the Pauline Gospel upon which the church had been established. Paul knew that if left unchecked, this perversion of the Gospel would lead to a lack of fruit in the lives of the believers. That's because in his mind, theology could never be separated from practical Christian living. So he pleaded with them in the strongest terms possible not to be taken captive by teachings and philosophies which, while sounding spiritual, were not according to Christ (Colossians 2:8).

Nowhere in this letter (or any other letter which he wrote) is there even a suggestion that what the church needed was revival to get them back on track. That is not to say that Paul didn't place great value on the power of the Spirit working in each community as a confirmation of the truth of the Gospel. Yet that is a far cry from the modern obsession with revival we often find in the Church today. For Paul, the working of the Spirit in each local church was always in *accordance* to a church's response to the Gospel (read the letter to the Galatians as evidence of this). Paul understood that when a community was faithful to the Gospel, it would result in the power of the Spirit working in their midst (Gal. 3:2-3).

Taking our cue from Paul has far reaching implications for the way we deal with local churches today. So often, when attempting to help churches in trouble, we tend to focus our attention on such things as the church's vision, financial health and commitment level among the members. Yet these are often symptomatic of the greater problem— the lack of a proper foundation in the biblical Gospel! If a church is not solidly built upon the Gospel, no adjustment in these other things will suffice in supplying what it lacks. That's because it is only when a church is built solidly on the truth of the Gospel that it can produce the fruit of the kingdom of God.

Theology on Fire

One idea which has gained in popularity today is that when revival comes there will be less need for preaching and teaching in the Church. This is one of those beliefs that is rarely spoken, yet it is not hard to detect. But I am convinced that it has greatly contributed to the demise of preaching in the Church today. After all, if preaching is only to be endured only until the power of the Spirit comes , it stands to reason that we may dispense with it whenever it suits us.

Yet this is another view which is not only contrary to Scripture, it ignores the plain facts of history. Whenever God has been pleased to send revival in the past it did not result in less preaching, but more! In fact, times of revival have actually empowered preachers to declare the Word with greater urgency than in normal seasons of church life. Some of the greatest preachers in American history, such as Jonathan Edwards and John Wesley, actually came to the forefront during times of great revival. Edwards himself preached one of this nation's most memorable sermons entitled "Sinners in the Hands of an Angry God" during the First Great Awakening. At the height of the revival in New England, God mightily anointed his messages so that hundreds were brought into the kingdom.

It might be helpful here if we reference Edwards' own view of revival during the Great Awakening. He referred to it as "theology on fire." Edwards firmly believed that both (*theology* and *fire*) were necessary components of true revival. For Edwards, *theology* was like the wood needed in order to have a fire—without it the fire cannot burn. *Fire* was the power of the Holy Spirit upon the preacher which made divine truth come alive. Edwards knew firsthand how the fire of the Holy Spirit enflamed theology so that lives were transformed. His messages were packed with theology so that not only were sinners brought to faith by them, they were used of God to sustain the saints as well.

Edwards' view of revival reveals one of the weaknesses of much revival thinking today. It focuses on fire while ignoring entirely the *wood* (theology). That came home to me a number of years ago while attending some meetings in our city where revival was purported to be happening. As I listened to the speakers over those days, I was amazed at the total absence of biblical preaching and teaching from the platform. Most of those speaking in those meetings spent their time telling of the various experiences they had in other revival meetings. There were numerous testimonies of miracles, but almost no exposition of the Word. The message was clear: when the Spirit is moving there is little need for biblical instruction.

I have no doubt that if Edwards had attended those meetings he would have protested vigorously, not because of the belief in miracles and healings purported to be happening, but the total absence of theological substance in the preaching. Reflecting on previous revivals, author John Armstrong points out how theology was always at the center of true revival:

> "When historian Gerald R. McDermott wrote a summary article on the evangelical awakening in America and Britain, he noted that 'the 18th-century awakening consisted of three massive revivals divided by an ocean, a sea, and thousands of miles.' He also observed that, though divided in the way, these revivals were all united by ten common characteristics. He noted as his third characteristic that 'revivals were sparked and sustained by the preaching of Reformation doctrines'" (John Armstrong, *When God Moves*, Harvest House, page 73, italics mine).

This is what sustained the 18th century revival and it is the only thing which will sustain true revival today as well. The preaching of God's Word must therefore be central to any genuine move of God. The idea that revival is a substitute for the proclamation of the Word of God is not only a departure from Scripture, it flies in the face of the clear record of history. In many eras of Church History, preaching itself was the catalyst which actually spawned revival:

> "A wave of authentic revival sweeps over the church when three things happen together: teaching the great truths of the gospel with

clarity, applying those truths to people's lives with spiritual power, and extending that experience to large numbers of people. We Evangelicals urgently need such an awakening today. We need to rediscover the gospel" (Raymond Ortlulo Evans, *Fire in the Hatch*, Bryntirion, Bridgend, Wales: Evangelical Press of Wales, 1996, page 29).

Writing to his young son in the faith, Paul urged Timothy to pay careful attention to both his *preaching* and *lifestyle* (I Timothy 4:16). For Paul, the preaching of the Gospel and godly living were not mere temporary aspects of ministry until revival comes, but the main components of pastoral ministry. Nowhere in the twin letters written to Timothy is there even a suggestion that he engage in preaching and teaching until the Holy Spirit moved on the churches in Asia. Rather, Timothy was to give himself to preaching both "in season and out of season" as the mainstay of a ministry faithful to God (II Timothy 4:2).

His Truth Goes Marching On

My desire in this chapter has not been to cast doubt on the reality of revival. It is clear from history that God does at times send powerful revivals upon his people. Yet we should not view these mighty outpourings of God's Spirit as a cure-all for what ails the Church. Rather, our hope must be in the Gospel as the ultimate provision of God to change both the Church as well as the culture.

One of the problems with the view that revival is the cure-all for all the Church's ills, is that it overlooks the relationship between the Spirit and the Word. It is true that it is the Holy Spirit who gives life to sinners and changes Christians, yet his main way of accomplishing that is by illuminating the God-breathed Scriptures, and applying them to our hearts so that we are forever changed. Any attempt, therefore, to set up an adversarial relationship between Word and Spirit is bogus. These two always work together in God's economy.

This fact (that Spirit and Word always work together) accounts for why we need an ongoing teaching ministry in the local church. Since the Gospel is not only the message we must hear in order to become Christians, but also the means by which we achieve sanctification as well, we must ensure that God's people are continually hearing it. Viewing the Gospel as the mere means of "getting us in" and not also the means of keeping us as well, greatly limits its power. The job of the local church, therefore, is to make sure God's people are continually hearing the Gospel.

Viewed in this light, the Church's theme song isn't "Blowin' in the Wind' but that old standard "His Truth Goes Marching On." The Church in every age is judged not by her experience of revival, but by her faithfulness to the truth of the Gospel. Revival comes and goes but the Word of the Lord remains forever! May His truth go marching on, ever conquering more and more hearts! Amen.

CHAPTER THREE

The Virtue of Unoriginality

Hang around the Body of Christ long enough, and you're bound to hear the word *postmodern* being bandied about. We are living in a *postmodern* culture with *postmoderns* who hold *postmodern* views and *postmodern* values. While scholars debate exactly what Postmodernism is, most agree it is now here in full force. And with it's arrival has come an entirely new way of looking at things! Gone are the old paradigms, having now been replaced by an entirely new set of ideals. Postmodernism has succeeded in changing the entire landscape of American life.

Sociologists and others who study human behavior believe the West has passed through three basic periods—the *Pre-modern, Modern,* and *Postmodern. The Pre-modern Era* is that period which preceded the scientific and social revolutions. It was largely characterized by religion, superstition, philosophy, mythology, tribalism, and feudalism with religion as its primary force. It comprised a wide range of speculative and superstitious beliefs, largely borrowed from the Greeks and Romans. The Pre-modern age was that period which gave rise to the great philosophers such as Plato, Aristotle, and Socrates. Even though their teachings were not biblical they laid the groundwork for Greek and Roman civilization and in the process, paved the way for biblical concepts to be more easily grasped when the Gospel arrived.

When the *Pre-modern* Age came to an end and the *Modern* began is anyone's guess. Some scholars suggest the eighteenth century Enlightenment as a good point of demarcation. The Enlightenment definitely signaled a radical change in the way men and women thought about themselves and their world. It was characterized by rapid advancement in knowledge in the realm of science and other areas. As knowledge grew, the sense of any need for God diminished as more and more people believed they could solve their problems on their own. Many moderns believed that freedom from God meant that man could build the perfect utopia by his own efforts. Not everyone, though, abandoned belief in God during the Modern Period. Some continued to speak of Him, not so much as a present Deity actively involved with His creation but as one far removed from this present world—sort of like a deadbeat father who after generating a family, subsequently abandons them. The technical term for this is *Deism;* the belief that God originally created all things, but then left His creatures to fend for themselves.

By the late eighteenth century Charles Darwin provided an explanation of the origin of species which made even the existence of God unnecessary. Not surprisingly, many who were formerly deists became atheists. Prior to the Enlightenment, Christianity was viewed as the embodiment of truth but with the profusion of knowledge now directly challenging the presuppositions of the faith, men and women began to question traditional beliefs, including various biblical accounts as such as creation, the flood, and the resurrection of Jesus. Free from their former slavery to the Christian worldview, men and women felt emboldened to pursue entirely different understandings of reality.

In the nineteenth century, Karl Marx developed his socialistic ideas around the premise that human beings had value *only* in relation to the masses. Marx abandoned the long cherished belief that man is a spiritual being and posited the notion that human beings could only be understood in terms of their *economic* or *social* status. *Socialism* eventually gave birth to *Communism* with its promise to eliminate all classes, thus creating the ideal utopia. Fifty years later, the entire project came crashing down, as one after another of the countries where the "glo-ries of socialism" had been tried began to embrace the values of the West. That's because any system which defines human beings solely in terms of economics or social class cannot stand, since it denies the most basic aspect of human existence—that human beings are incur-ably moral and spiritual.

Some scholars and historians believe the collapse of Communism signaled the end of *Modernism* and the beginning of the *Postmodern* Age. It is difficult to pinpoint when such a momentous shift in the culture took place. What is clear, is that the West entered headlong into a new way of looking at things. Paramount to this new way of thinking was the abandonment of *absolutism*—the belief that absolute truth exists and can be objectively known. The result was then *relativism*—that all philosophical and moral systems are essentially the same, and there-fore are to be tolerated. This includes religion, as long as its adherents refrain from any insistence that others should believe as well (appar-ently this is the only absolute which is to be tolerated).

One way of understanding how each period differs from the other is by examining their attitude towards absolute truth. Author Os Gui-ness uses a helpful analogy by comparing these three periods to three baseball umpires describing their philosophy of umpiring a game.[1] The Pre-modern umpire describes his philosophy this way—"There's balls and there's strikes, and I call them the way they *are*." Notice his philoso-phy of umpiring; he simply calls them "the way they *are*." This reflects the Pre-Modern view that absolute truth exists, and that we must simply recognize it. The umpire representing the *Modern Era* has a slightly dif-ferent philosophy of umpiring a game: "There's balls and there's strikes, I call them the way I *see* them." This umpire introduces the *subjective* ele-ment—he "calls them the way he *sees* them." This accords perfectly with the subjectivity which characterized much of the Modern Age. Whereas in the Pre-modern age the idea of absolute truth was accepted without

---

1. The story of the Three Umpires is taken from the book "Time for Truth" by Os Guinness

question, the Modern Age adopted the view that truth is determined by how each individual *sees* it rather than how it actually *is*.

The third umpire describes his philosophy of umpiring this way: "there's balls and there's strikes, and they're nothing till I call them!" This represents the radical *relativistic* view of the Postmodern Age and its wholesale abandonment of the idea of absolute truth. For Post-moderns, the individual determines what is true (there's nothing till I call them!". Relativism is the view that truth is relative to each person rather than something objective each person must recognize.

A New Kind of Christian

In recent years, several Christian authors have addressed the challenge Postmodernism presents to biblical faith. While some have pointed out it's inherent dangers, others have called attention to the fact that Postmodernism affords the church of God with incredible opportunities for kingdom expansion, but only if the local church itself becomes thoroughly *postmodern*. Their call (that the local church itself become thoroughly postmodern if it desires to reach a postmodern culture) is now arising from many quarters. One of the most popular authors in this regard is Brian MacLaren. In a popular work entitled *A New Kind of Christian*, MacLaren draws from the experiences of nine individual believers each of whom failed to be ministered to by the local church. His conclusion is that the failure of the Church to minister effectively to these people is evidence that the Church is hopelessly wedded to the past, and therefore unable to effectively minister to Postmoderns. This leads MacLaren to ask the following questions; "Doesn't the religious community have anything fresh and incisive to say? Isn't it even asking any new questions? Has it nothing to offer other than the stock formulas that it has been offering?"

These questions set up the basic premise of the book; that the Church must produce a "new kind of Christian"—a *postmodern* Christian if it hopes to be effective in ministering to a postmodern world. To buttress this argument MacLaren cites the example of several persons in Church history such as Francis of Assisi and C.S. Lewis whom he says constituted a "new kind of Christian" in their day. He praises them for being innovators who brought fresh ideas on the scene at a time when it was desperately needed. In the remainder of the book, MacLaren contends that it is only as the Church produces this 'new kind of Christian' that it can hope to be effective in ministering to the culture.

Not all have accepted willy-nilly this call for the Church to become thoroughly postmodern. In an article in Christianity Today entitled *The Virtue of Unoriginality*, Mark Galli, after reviewing MacLaren's book, takes issue with his basic premise. Galli acknowledges that MacLaren's work is helpful in providing his readers with keen cultural analysis. But Galli takes it to task for its assertion that the only hope for the Church is the emergence of a *new* kind of Christian. He reminds his readers that the Church's success in any age has not come by studying the culture and then tailoring its approach to cultural norms, but by maintaining its historic commitment to Scripture. According to Galli, the Church's most successful times were always started with a fresh rediscovery of the power of the Word of God:

> "Nearly every agent of church renewal began by comparing the church or himself not with the intellectual and cultural trends but with the faith of the ages, particularly biblical teaching. The monastic movement began when Anthony of the Desert heard Matthew 19-21 read in Church. The Reformation began when Luther, after years of internal struggles, finally understood Romans 1:16. The Pentecostal Movement took off because people believed they were living again in apostolic times, in which Acts 2 was a living reality" (*The Virtue of Unoriginality*, Christianity Today).

For Galli, those movements which deeply impacted culture first began with a deep engagement of Scripture. MacLaren's book (according to Galli) fails precisely because it ignores this fact. By saying something *more* than the "stock phrases of Scripture" is needed, MacLaren fails to realize that those who changed society in the past knew that there was nothing so fresh and incisive as those so-called "stock phrases of Scripture." Luther and Saint Francis of Assisi left their mark on their day precisely because of their unswerving commitment to the Word of God.

At one point in MacLaren's book he asks the question, "Has the good news been reduced to the "good same-old same old?" Yet it has been the historic Church's commitment to this "good same-old same old" which accounts for its effectiveness in ages past. And it will only be as the Church remains faithful to the "good same-old same old" in the future that it will continue to further the purpose of God in the earth.

Ancient Landmarks and Old Wineskins

I once heard a good friend of mine, Jim McCracken, preach a message in which he talked about the failure of believers to distinguish between 'ancient landmarks' and 'old wineskins.' By 'ancient landmarks' Jim referred to the eternal truth of God contained in Scripture. Even though it is *ancient* (spoken long ago through apostles and prophets) it is never *antiquated* but always relevant for the Church in every age. His reference to Scripture as a 'landmark' was drawn from the Old Testament regulation forbidding Israelites from moving landmarks in the allotting of territory in the land of Israel. In the same way the Israelites were forbidden to move landmarks, so the Church is forbidden from changing the written revelation of God.

In the message, Jim reminded us that wineskins in Scripture are representative of structures and ways of doing things. This is how Jesus used it in the well-known parable about putting "new wine into new wineskins" (Matt. 9:17). The immediate context of Jesus' teaching was that the new wine Jesus brought by his coming could not be contained in the old structures of Judaism—there would have to be new forms to contain it (new wineskins). Jesus had come to bring the new wine of the kingdom and it was not possible for the Judaism of his day to contain it.

This applies, of course, not only to first century Jews but to us as well who must recognize the difference between ancient landmarks and old wineskins. Very often, churches end up defending to the death the way we do things, yet show very little concern that the truth of Scripture is being trampled on. They are either totally committed to the ancient landmarks (Scripture) while ignoring wineskins altogether, or else they are totally focused on wineskins (ways of doing things) and ignore the truth of Scripture altogether. I have personally known churches who should be commended for their commitment to biblical truth, yet who resist tooth and nail any changes in the way they do things. They have become in fact "old wineskins." On the other hand, I have also known churches that were so afraid of becoming *old* wineskins they willingly embraced everything new coming down the pike for fear that if they didn't, they might miss entirely what God was doing.

Is it possible for a church to be thoroughly committed to the historic Gospel yet avoid becoming an 'old wineskin?' I believe it is. In fact, I am convinced that this is the specific challenge facing many churches today. Congregations and leaders must realize that while methods and ways of doing things will often change, the truth of God never does. That means when it comes to methods and ways of doing things we must be willing to change whenever they no longer suit our purpose. Yet when it comes to our commitment to the historic Gospel, we must be fiercely immovable. That's because it has always been the historic Church's commitment to the truth of the Gospel which accounts for her ability to change the culture. As Mark Galli stated in his article those who have been most effective in their generation are those who understood that while the outward aspects of ministry may change as culture change, their commitment to the eternal truth of God must never waver.

The challenge Postmodernism presents to the Church is certainly real but it must reinvigorate us so that we commit ourselves to the historic Gospel, life-changing Gospel of God. When it comes to our commitment to the historic Gospel God has called us to be gloriously *unoriginal*. But when it comes to our wineskins, we can be as flexible as we need to be.

What Lies Ahead

My aim in this first section was to highlight some of the reasons for the loss of passion for truth in the Church today. We looked at three that have contributed greatly to the loss of passion for truth; a preoccupation with experiences, popular ideas regarding revival, and our response to living in a *Postmodern* age. While many other things could have been considered in this section, these are critical for understanding why there has been a general loss of passion for truth in the Church of God today.

Yet there is still another reason for the loss of passion for truth in the Church today. I consider it to be so important I have devoted the entirety of the next section to it. It is the total confusion in much of the Church today regarding the place of the *mind* in the Christian life. An increasing *anti-intellectualism* characterizes much of the Church today, and this has had a devastating effect on the development of Christian spirituality. When speaking of anti-intellectualism, I refer to the increasing *mindlessness* characterizing much of Postmodern culture including the Church of Jesus Christ. While what often passes for Christian spirituality today encourages people to pursue experiences with God, it often ignores entirely the necessity of developing the mind as an important aspect of Christian discipleship.

What is desperately needed today is for a new generation of believers to emerge who know the importance of *thinking* to the glory of God. Yet first they must rid themselves of many of the false notions concerning the mind in vogue in much of the Church world today. In the next section, we will examine some of these false ideas that will have to be abandoned if a restoration of passion for truth in the people of God is to be a reality.

A MINDLESS FAITH

CHAPTER FOUR

A Mind is a Terrible Thing to Waste

I briefly referred, in the previous section, to my first experience of church life in a small church in Miami Beach, Florida. Possessed with an insatiable desire to learn all I could about my new Christian faith, I entered the church eager to get started. I came to each church service ready to absorb our pastor's fiery sermons. Our pastor laid particular emphasis in those days on the importance of discipline in the Christian life. It was during those early days that I first learned about the things I should regularly practice in order to become a fruitful believer, such as personal prayer, Bible reading, fasting, and sharing my faith with others. It was during those days that I first shared my personal testimony at evangelistic street campaigns organized by our church. I am thankful for the disciplines I learned in those early days. Many of them have remained with me now for over thirty years.

One discipline I didn't learn in those days, though, was the importance of disciplining my mind as a follower of Jesus Christ. I cannot remember hearing even one message about the importance of *thinking* as a believer. Looking at many of the members of my church, it was not difficult to understand why this vital topic was ignored. I got the impression from observing them that spirituality had little to do with the mind, but was rather mostly concerned with the cultivation of certain emotions, and pursuing spiritual experiences. Since few in our church seemed concerned about disciplining their minds, I concluded that the development of my mind must not be important when it came to being a disciple. Consequently, I ignored the growth of my intellect, and pursued these other things.

This worked fine for a while, but before long I found myself totally bored (intellectually) with what my church had to offer. While I continued to appreciate my pastor's fiery messages calling us to a life of consecration, I found myself hungry for a faith which was *intellectually* satisfying, as well as emotionally satisfying. I had an insatiable desire to learn all I could about the Word of God and theology, yet few in our church seemed interested in such pursuits. It soon became apparent that if I was to awaken my brain to learn, I would basically have to go it alone.

That was discouraging at first but it actually turned out to be a blessing in disguise. It forced me to develop new study habits and stretch my mind to learn. It was at that time that I began reading challenging theological books in order to put myself in a growth mode. Some of these were quite difficult at first, and I was tempted to give up. Yet I learned that by perseverance, I had a much greater capacity to learn than I gave myself credit for. The most amazing thing I discovered was that as I awakened my mind, my entire Christian life was being renewed!

Since that time I have made this emphasis (the need to awaken our minds) a vital one in my own ministry. I believe it is much needed in the Church today. Few believers are being taught the importance of developing their minds as an integral part of their life with God. In fact, many are actually being taught that the mind is a hindrance to the development of Christian spirituality, and that the way to achieve spirituality is by "getting out of their minds."

Why is the vital place the mind holds in the Christian life so denigrated in much of the Church today? For one, many believers have been taught things contrary to Scripture when it comes to the intellect. The result has been the emergence of a sort of *mindless* Christianity masking as Christian spirituality. Believers have been taught that they must choose between "living in the mind" on the one hand, or "living in the Spirit" on the other. These being the choices, who wouldn't choose living in the Spirit every time?

As I will try to demonstrate in this section, that is a bogus "choice." This is because life in the Spirit requires the fullest use of the mind. There is no doubt that these (and other) wrong ideas regarding the mind in the Christian life have singlehandedly contributed to a number of deficiencies in Christian living. Not the least of these deficiencies, is the waning desire among God's people to engage in serious study of the Word of God. Since understanding God's truth in Scripture requires the fullest workings of the mind, the undermining of intellectual development has destroyed incentive to deeply penetrate Scripture. It is not surprising therefore that our churches are filled with mentally lazy believers who leave serious study of God's Word to the so-called experts.

The remainder of this chapter will focus on understanding how God intended *rationality* as the primary means of reflecting the image of the God who made us. Chapter five entitled *Transformed by the Removing of Your Mind* looks at the effect mindlessness has had on many of our ideas of Christian discipleship. Chapter six, *The Cure for Boredom with God* is an analysis of why there is so much boredom with God in the Church today, recommending as its cure what many see as the reason for the boredom: *theology*. Finally, Chapter seven, *Enjoying God Without Losing Your Mind* looks at the relationship between *thinking* and *feeling* as exemplified in those forgotten saints of a bygone era; the English Puritans.

Mindlessness and Meaninglessness

Dr. John Stott tells the story of two women who were friends and ran into each other in a supermarket one day. As they spoke, one of the women noticed that her friend seemed quite upset. "What is the matter with you," she asked, "You look so worried." "I am," her friend replied.

"I've been thinking about the world situation." "Well then," her friend said, "You ought to take things more philosophically and *stop thinking*."

According to Dr. Stott the counsel the woman offered her friend in the supermarket that day to "take things more philosophically and stop thinking" represents the *mindlessness* evident in much of the Western world today. It is analogous to what many have come to believe; that the way to become more philosophical is by *neglecting* the mind rather than developing it. When people speak of the "good life" today, they usually are referring to the condition of their material, emotional, or relational life, not the state of their intellectual life.

Dr. Stott went on to say that wherever mindlessness exists, her twin sister *meaninglessness* is not far behind. That's because whenever people succumb to the notion that achieving the better life requires them to "turn off the mind", an inevitable loss of meaning follows. This accounts for why so many in the culture today have drifted towards *existentialism* (the belief that the universe has no intrinsic meaning or purpose and that each person must determine his or her own meaning). Having lost the capacity for critical thinking, they easily drift into meaningless existences.

A few years ago I had an opportunity to talk to a relative about my faith in God. Since I had never spoken to her about spiritual things before I began by asking her some basic questions about her life in order to ascertain her values and life goals. It soon became apparent that she had not given much thought to her life apart from the incidentals such as working, sleeping, eating and playing. Apart from these things she could offer no real reason for being alive. Needless to say, the conversation didn't go very far.

Sadly, my relative is typical of many in the culture today who live without any real sense of purpose or meaning. Despite the fact that we live at a time in which we have unlimited access to knowledge, a deep sense of meaninglessness now pervades much of Western culture. Many have forgotten (or never learned) that without intellectual stimulation, the mere accumulation of knowledge will not fill their lives with purpose and meaning. Purpose and meaning can only be achieved by exercising the mind to the fullest so as to begin to understand who we are and why we are here.

God's Purpose For Our Minds

In the first two chapters of Genesis we learn the important place God gave to the mind when he created human beings in his image and likeness. From the beginning, God endowed humans with *rationality* as the major means of reflecting their likeness to the Creator. It is this which separates us from the animal kingdom in God's creation order. To human beings alone was given a complex ability to reason and thereby understand the world which He created.

Many Bible readers assume that the statement in Genesis that God created man "in His own image and likeness" refers to the fact that we are *spiritual* in nature; that God endowed the human spirit with the innate capacity for direct communion with God apart from the mind. Others, seeing no reason to limit it to the spiritual alone, argue that it includes our physical frame as well. According to this view, since the Lord Jesus Christ Himself existed in a physical form before His incarnation, He served as a prototype for the way in which God fashioned our own bodies.

While both of these views have merit, they fail to capture the real essence of what is meant by our having been created in God's "image and likeness." It is not primarily the *spiritual* or *physical* aspects of our being which reflect the divine image but *rationality*—our innate ability to exercise our minds so as to understand both our Creator and the world He created. This rationality most reflects our being like our Creator. In saying this I am not negating the importance of our physical and spiritual faculties. I am saying that this incredible capacity to reason is the most powerful way in which we reflect our likeness to our Creator. When when we use this capacity to the fullest, we bring glory to the God who made us in His image and likeness.

One writer who understood this well was the great Puritan theologian John Owen. His writings reveal his depth of insight regarding the place God gave the intellect at creation. According to Owen, all of the other faculties of volition and emotion were created to work in concert with the intellect:

> "God created them all in a perfect harmony and union. The mind and the reason were in perfect subjection and subordination to God and his will; the will answered, in its choice of good, the discovery made of it by the mind, the affections constantly and evenly followed the understanding and will." (*Overcoming Sin and Temptation*, John Owen, pg 253)

Notice how this perfect harmony existing between the faculties found its balance in the mind. Prior to the Fall, the mind was "in perfect subjection and subordination to God and his will." In other words, the mind took the lead in discovering what pleased God and the other faculties followed suit. A breakdown of the interplay of these faculties at creation, as understood by Owen, is as follows:

- the mind led in discovering God's will
- the will chose the good which the mind discovered
- the emotions delighted in what the mind discovered and the will chose

For Owen, *rationality* was the primary faculty by which humans expressed the divine image. That meant that by exercising their intellects to the fullest, human beings brought glory to their Creator. The animal world was also created to bring glory to God but they did so *unconsciously*. Humans, on the other hand, were created to *consciously* reflect God's glory. That is why King David, when reflecting upon the wonder of how he was made, declared he was "fearfully and wonderfully made" (Psalm 139:14). When we consider the amazing way in which we are made, we also will praise Him for our having been created as *rational* beings.

One group which understood this were the early pioneers of the scientific revolution. They saw no contradiction between their faith in God and rational exploration of the universe, viewing both as attempts at gaining knowledge of God. The English philosopher Sir Francis Bacon, who first proposed a theory of scientific knowledge based on observation and experiment known as the inductive method, said that God had actually written two books—the book of *nature* and the book of *Scripture*. According to Bacon the book of nature revealed his *glory* while the book of Scripture revealed his *grace*. Since both were from God, he could easily pass from one to the other, viewing science as the attempt to understand and systematize what God had revealed in nature, while theology was the attempt to understand and systematize what God had revealed in Scripture.

What propelled these early scientific pioneers was their belief that the universe was an intelligible system which could be properly understood through investigation. Since God had made the universe this way, a close correspondence existed between the mind of the investigator (the scientist) and that which he was investigating (the universe). Albert Einstein is once reported to have said, "The only incomprehensible thing about the universe is that it is comprehensible—we can understand it!" This belief in the rationality of the universe accounts for why many of these early scientific pioneers believed that by investigating the universe, they were glorifying the Creator. German astronomer Johannes Kepler, considered by many to be the founder of modern astronomy, once said that when seeking to understand the universe, we are "thinking God's thoughts after Him." Far from believing that the pursuit of scientific knowledge would take him away from God (as many modern scientists do), Kepler considered his work to be a means of gaining a greater understanding of the Creator.

Yet while these scientists believed the universe yielded important clues as to who God was, they also believed it (creation) was not sufficient in providing an understanding of salvation through Jesus Christ. For that God wrote a second book—the book of *Scripture*, in which He revealed his grace through the redemptive work of His Son, Christ Jesus. While the book of nature provides us with *general* knowledge of

God and is available to all, the revelation contained in Scripture is *special*. It gives us knowledge of what God has accomplished through the death and resurrection of His Son which we could not know otherwise unless God had revealed it to us.

What these scientists have discovered is in full accord with the Genesis account of creation. God had purposed from the beginning that human beings glorify Him through the exercise of their reasoning powers. Upon their initial creation Adam and Eve did not have at their disposal all the knowledge they needed of God, or their world, or even of themselves. God had ordained for them to obtain this knowledge only through diligent study and exploration. That is why he endowed them with rationality, so they could exercise their minds in a never-ending exploration of both Him and all that He had made. In this manner they were to fulfill their destiny.

The Loss of a Christian Mind

Since God created us with rationality, it follows that He expects us to use it to the fullest. Any attempt to demean the intellect distorts the image of God in man. Mindlessness, therefore, is a direct assault on the God who created us in His own image and likeness.

Yet our culture today continues to celebrate mindlessness. As I stated earlier in this chapter, "the good life" is rarely portrayed today as having to do with the life of the mind but is largely focused on the cultivation of the physical and emotional life. Intellectuals are typically not cast as the most exciting people in the world.

Sadly, mindlessness is not only endemic of the culture at large, but also of much of the Church of Jesus Christ as well. Today, there has been a general "dumbing down of the Church." Whereas the Church once turned out the greatest thinkers, it now produces people who are largely *secularized* in their thinking. English author Harry Blamires in his classic book *The Christian Mind* accurately describes the loss of the Christian mind in the community of faith:

"There is no longer a Christian mind. There is still, of course, a Christian ethic, a Christian practice, and a Christian spirituality. As a moral being, the modern Christian suscribes to a code other than that of the non-Christian. As a member of the church, he undertakes obligations and observations ignored by the non-Christian. As a spiritual being, in prayer and meditation, he strives to cultivate a dimension of life unexplored by the non-Christian. But as a thinking being, the modern Christian has succumbed to secularization. He accepts religion—its morality, its worship, its spiritual culture; but he rejects the religious view of life, the view which sets all earthly issues within the context of the eternal, the view which relates all human problems—social, political, cultural—to the doctrinal foundations of the Christian Faith, the view which sees all things here below in terms of God's supremacy and earth's transitoriness in terms of Heaven and Hell."

According to Blamires, a Christian mind is not a mind which thinks only about Christian things, but one able to think clearly about *all* things from a Christian perspective. While many Christians today can converse freely about religious matters, they are often unable to talk about things such as politics, sex, nuclear proliferation, or education from a Christian perspective. In fact, many Christians avoid thinking or conversing on these topics altogether, having bought into the notion that such things are *worldly*. For them, the sanctified person should think only about so-called *spiritual* things. So, rather than engaging the culture intellectually, the Church has dropped out of the intellectual fray and in so doing, has lost a major means of confronting the culture with the Gospel.

One clear evidence of this mindlessness in the Church today is the promulgation of the so-called 'simple' Gospel. Having capitulated to the culture, we have constructed a Gospel requiring very little intellectual involvement. But we have failed to realize that there is a profound difference between the 'simple' Gospel and a 'simplistic' Gospel, shorn of all intellectual substance. Judging from much of what passes for evangelism in the Church today with its emphasis on room atmospherics and the telling of stories rather than presenting clearly structured arguments for the Gospel, it would appear this simplistic Gospel is now firmly in place.

A number of years ago I was invited to speak in a fairly large church on a Sunday morning. As I was delivering the message I sensed that many of the people were unable to grasp what I was saying, even though the subject I was teaching that morning was not particularly difficult. Still, I was very aware that people were struggling to understand me. I thought that the problem was with me—perhaps I had not adequately prepared my message or prayed enough for the engagement. Yet, as I reflected upon my preparation for this engagement, I realized that I had given the same amount of time to prayer and study as I normally did. So I was confused as to why I was not connecting with the people.

As my wife and I were leaving the church at the conclusion of the service I asked her if she had sensed my struggle to deliver the word. She said that she had, but then immediately said something which helped me to understand the reason for my struggle: "The sad truth is, these people are *brain dead*." She was not intending to be unkind by this statement, but was simply pointing out that these believers had never really been challenged to think deeply. Therefore, when I came into their midst and spoke to them on a level requiring them to exercise their minds, they were unable to do so, and were therefore hindered from receiving the message.

Sadly, that church is typical of many churches today; churches which might best be described by the motto, "Big *Hearts*: Small *Minds*." Having accepted the notion that true spirituality has little to do with the mind, many churches today foster notions of spirituality which are not only contrary to Scripture, but contradict the plain facts of history as well. Church history is replete with examples of passionate believers like St. Augustine and Jonathan Edwards, who exercised their minds to the fullest in their pursuit of God while at the same time passionately pursuing God Himself. The reason they were passionate was they believed that the mind was crucial in the development of real passion for God.

Often, when speaking to believers about the importance of developing their minds as a vital component of their pursuit of God, I get blank stares. It simply has not occurred to many people that the mind really matters when it comes to spiritual things. They have viewed the passionate life in terms of the display of emotion, rather than the exercise of the intellect. By so doing they have failed to understand the close correspondence which exists between the mind and the emotions. I will deal with this much more in depth in the last chapter of this section.

Without a doubt, the most important area where believers must develop their minds is in the whole arena of Christian discipleship. Usually, believers focus on the will and emotions, ignoring the mind entirely when it comes to developing a life of discipleship. But this is a real mistake, as I will seek to establish in the next chapter. One of the great needs for believers therefore, is to return to a biblical view of Christian discipleship which includes the cultivation of the intellect as a major aspect of our following Christ. Yet, if we are going to be successful in that endeavor, we will first have to rid ourselves of some of the unscriptural notions regarding the mind. This we will attempt do in the next chapter.

CHAPTER FIVE

Transformed by the *Removing* of Your Mind

Anyone serious about living the Christian life must eventually grapple with Paul's words in Romans 12:1-2 (Therefore I urge you, brethren, by the mercies of God, to present your bodies a living and holy sacrifice, acceptable to God, which is your spiritual service of worship. And do not be conformed to this world, but be transformed by the renewing of your mind, so that you may prove what the will of God is, that which is good and acceptable and perfect). In two short verses the apostle gives the Roman church a description of normative Christian consecration, which serves as a defining statement of how he views the Christian life. It is not a description of some extraordinary level of spiritual living only for elite Christians, but rather a description of the basic requirements of discipleship for all who would follow Jesus. To quote Paul's own words, it is our *"reasonable* service" (Romans 12:1, KJV, italics mine).

Looking carefully at Paul's words, it becomes apparent that he views the renewed *mind* as the central organ of the transformed life. The disciple of Christ must no longer be "conformed to this world" but be "transformed" by the *renewing* of the mind. According to the apostle, it is through the complete renewal of the mind that the ideals of the new life are properly lived out. At face value these words reinforce the important place which God gives to the mind in the Christian life. Yet despite this clear teaching of the apostle, many believers today continue to view the mind as a hindrance rather than an aid to achieving Christian spirituality. Many churches actually teach their members that the mind should be ignored rather than developed. It is not surprising therefore that our churches are packed with people who have not learned that the pathway to the passionate life is *through* the mind.

After first entering church life in my church in Miami, I got the impression from observing people in the church that developing my mind was the least important thing I should be concerned with. The message I seemed to receive upon entering was, "Come on in and park your brain at the door; you won't be needing it here." After a year or two in the church I thought Romans 12:2 actually read "be transformed by the removing of your mind" rather than the "renewing of your mind."

Much later, after studying the passage more fully, I realized that Paul is actually calling for the full renewal of the mind rather than its removal. That meant that, far from calling me to the kind of mindlessness I found in my church, this passage actually called for the fullest exercise of my mind. Further study of this passage in Romans yielded incredible insights. I discovered that the Greek word translated by the English word "transformed" ("do not be conformed to this world but be transformed") is metamorphizo, the word from which we derive our English word metamorphosis. Metamorphosis refers to the transformation of a species from one form to another such as when a caterpillar turns into a butterfly. The same word is used in the Gospel of Luke regarding the alteration of Jesus' physical appearance on the Mount of Transfiguration. At that time, the body of Jesus underwent a complete change as He was glorified (Luke 9:29). When used in Romans 12:2 in connection with our minds it depicts the radical change which should result from true Christian sanctification. The believer who offers to God his body is to undergo a complete transformation of character beginning with a metamorphosis of the mind.

In light of this clear teaching of Scripture, why do so many believers continue to hold to the notion that the mind is a hindrance to following Jesus? I believe it is due to the fact that much Christian teaching and literature on the market today, subtly (and not so subtly) denigrates the mind. It portrays disciples as those engaged in certain activities, or who have had certain experiences, rather than those who are steadily improving their minds. Activities such as prayer, fasting, and other spiritual disciplines are deemed to be more important than meditation and study.

This has resulted in a general mindlessness throughout much of the Christian church which has not only affected the typical member, but many pastors and church leaders as well. Few take time today to regularly engage in deeper study of the Scriptures or theology. While it is true that the average pastor today is given little time for such activities, the real reason for the lack of intellectual engagement of many leaders today is not the lack of time, but the general belief that enhancing the mind through arduous study is of little value when compared to other activities. If those called to feed the flock of God spend little time exercising their minds, why should those they lead bother to do so?

In this chapter I examine the ways in which mindlessness has affected many of our present ideas regarding Christian discipleship in the Church today. Time will not allow for a thorough examination of all the areas affected by mindlessness. Here, I focus specifically on three which are central to living fruitful Christian lives: faith, divine guidance and evangelism. By examining these three, we will have a better understanding of the way in which mindlessness has hindered our living as fruitful disciples of Jesus Christ.

Faith

No area of Christian discipleship is more important than *faith*. The writer of Hebrews tells us that "without faith it is impossible to please God" (Hebrews 11:6). The Christian life from start to finish is a life of faith (Romans 1:17). Faith is an indispensable element of Christian discipleship.

Since faith is such an important component of Christian living, it is not surprising that there is a great profusion of teaching on the subject throughout the Church today. Yet not all who teach about faith are agreed on what it is. Some teach that faith is essentially a belief in things that cannot possibly be verified—what is commonly known as 'blind' faith. According to this view, faith and reason are antithetical so that the person with faith can never depend on his or her reasoning powers. Such a view is often found where people who are freshly coming to Jesus are told by counselors to put aside their minds by just "accepting Jesus into their hearts." To bolster this view of faith, Solomon's words in Proverbs 3:5 are often quoted: "Trust in the Lord with all your heart and *lean not* to your own understanding." Supposedly, Solomon is teaching here that trusting God (faith) and reasoning are in radical opposition, and therefore the believer must choose between them.

Yet upon closer inspection it is clear that Solomon is not at all teaching that our reasoning powers are in opposition to trusting God, but rather is reminding us that we are finite, and therefore must not depend on our understanding *alone*, since God is greater than our understanding. We are to trust Him even when we don't understand what He is doing. It is not reasoning therefore which Solomon condemns, but pride.

Elsewhere in Scripture we learn that it is not reasoning which is the opposite of faith but *sight* (II Corinthians. 5:7). Believers are to treat invisible realities as though they are real even though they can't see them. We can do this precisely because God has supplied us with an understanding of these realities in his Word. Elsewhere, Solomon says that "it is the glory of God to conceal a matter, but the glory of kings to search it out" (Proverbs 25:2). As believer-priests we are to exercise our minds to the fullest in order to understand what God has revealed in his Word. Yet we do so with the awareness that we are finite and will never understand *all* of God's ways. We will have to content ourselves with what He has chosen to reveal.

I once heard a description of faith from Dr. John Stott which really captures the biblical idea. He referred to it as a "reasoning trust."

He derived this description from a statement from David in one of his Psalms: "those who know your name will trust in you" (Psalm 9:10). Notice how David draws a close relationship between what a person knows and their ability to trust. They trust precisely because they know! In other words, it is their personal knowledge of God that serves as the basis for their ability to trust God. That is why Dr Stott referred to it as a "reasoning trust."

Devotional writers are quick to point out that the word know in this text and in many other passages throughout the Old Testament refers to much more than mere intellectual knowledge, but to personal, experiential knowledge of God as well. While that is true, we must always remember that personal knowledge of God is never gained apart from a cognitive knowledge of God's Word. Knowledge of God gained through Scripture actually enables our faith to experience Him more completely and trust Him more fully.

I once read a story which vividly describes how knowledge of God gained from Scripture enables and encourages faith. Dr. John Piper tells about a certain couple in his church who discovered that one of their children had been repeatedly molested. At the time they learned of this awful fact, Dr. Piper was engaged in teaching a series in his church on the nature and attributes of God. After several weeks of preaching messages from this series, the couple told him of their child's molestation. While they told him how devastated they were they also told him that the thing which had sustained them during the ordeal was the exalted view of God they had gleaned from his messages. Even though those messages did not deal directly with their situation, their faith was strengthened as they came to know God in a greater way through the written Word.

Divine Guidance

Another area of Christian discipleship adversely affected by mindlessness is that of divine *guidance;* understanding the way in which God directs his children. The fact that God does guide His own seems to be the clear teaching of Scripture. Nevertheless, not all believers are agreed as to exactly how such guidance is given.

Some believers, for example, take a so-called supernatural approach to divine guidance. They believe that God guides his own primarily through supernatural means such as dreams, visions, and inner voices. Because of this they are often reticent to make decisions until they have had a supernatural experience of some kind indicating what they should do. This was the view that I learned as a new believer, mainly by observing other believers in my church. Some spoke of hearing God tell them what restaurant to eat at or what person to marry or what car to buy. A woman in our church even claimed that God told her what color blouse to wear in the morning! In the entire time I was in that church, I cannot recall even once hearing someone say that God had directed them through the normal processes of the mind. The clear impression I received was that the mind was unimportant (even a hindrance) when it came to receiving divine guidance.

I am firmly convinced by Scripture that God does lead his children supernaturally whenever He so chooses. In the book of Acts there are numerous examples of God leading His people supernaturally. What is often overlooked though, is that these incidents of supernatural guidance were often separated by months or even years. So this is clearly not the normal way in which God guides His people. Nevertheless, I see nothing in Scripture to indicate that He no longer guides His people at times in this fashion. Besides being Scriptural, I myself have been the recipient of supernatural guidance.

In reaction to the unfortunate extremes, some believers reject all notions of supernatural guidance, choosing rather to believe that God *only* guides His people in this dispensation through the Scriptures. They look with suspicion on those claiming any supernatural experience of guidance, feeling that it weakens the sufficiency of Scripture. Since (according to this view) Scripture is totally sufficient, the believer never needs anything else for divine guidance. As I stated previously I see nothing in Scripture that precludes God from leading us supernaturally when He so chooses. Still, we should appreciate this emphasis on the sufficiency of Scripture as pertains to divine guidance.

The best description of divine guidance in all of Scripture is actually found right here in Romans 12:2. In this text Paul draws a clear connection between the renewed mind and the ability to 'prove' God's will. It is only as our minds are thoroughly renewed, that we can understand what God expects of us. Far from being a hindrance therefore, the renewed mind is actually essential to knowing and doing the will of God. That means that the more our minds are renewed, the greater will be our ability to understand God's will in every area of our lives.

The connection between the renewed mind and the ability to do God's will becomes clearer when we understand exactly what the apostle means by "will of God" in this passage. Many assume that when Scripture speaks of the will of God it is referring to the so-called *incidentals* of life—what college we should attend, or what person we should marry, or what job we should take. But that is not at all what the biblical phrase "will of God" means. This phrase also means what has often been called the "moral" aspect of God's will; that aspect of God's will which informs as to how we should live and please God. Author Gary Friesen helps us to understand this aspect of God's will:

> "The 12th chapter of Romans marks the beginning of the second major section of the epistle. The first eleven chapters contain a closely argued exposition of doctrine. Chapters 12 through 16 follow through with exhortations regarding appropriate behavior that corresponds to the doctrine taught. In Romans 12:1, Paul is saying on the basis of God's mercies, which have just been explained in detail, surrender your body to God for obedient living. Then, beginning with verse three, and extending on into the next four chapters, he spells out the commands that ought to be obeyed. In other words, as soon as he completes his exhortation to "prove what the will of God is," he begins giving specific examples of that will. Significantly, they are moral commands addressed to all believers. The immediate context says nothing about such things as finding one's vocation, choosing one's mate, or anything else that is so specific as to be part of God's individual will.

Rather, there are commands concerning the use of one's gifts (12:10), diligence in serving the Lord (12:11), rejoicing (12:12), hospitality (12:13), blessing persecutors (12:14) and so on. These obviously reflect the moral rather than the individual will of God" (Gary Friesen, *Decision Making and the Will of God*, Multnomah, page 106).

Friesen's distinction between the moral will of God and the individual will of God is an important one. Much of the confusion in the Body of Christ today regarding God's will comes from the idea that in all our decisions we must seek for a personal communication of God's will on the matter. As Friesen points out, this is not what Paul is teaching in this passage. Rather, he is referring to the moral will of God— learning to discern the things that are pleasing to God. The practical effect of this is, as we become progressively more acquainted with the moral will of God, it informs us in all of our decisions regarding the so-called "incidentals" of life.

I have found this distinction to be especially helpful whenever I help someone who has been agonizing over finding God's will in a certain matter. By the time they came to me they were often in despair as to whether they would ever find God's will. I usually begin by asking that person a simple question: "What is your preference in this matter?" People are often totally caught off guard by this question. It simply never occurred to them that God may have already put in their heart a desire to do what He wanted. By asking them what they wanted in the matter I hoped to assist them in realizing that God expected them to use their sanctified minds to determine His will for their lives.

One of the most liberating things we will ever discover is that God leaves many of the decisions we have to make in this life up to us. It is our responsibility, though, to ensure that the decisions we make are being informed by his moral will for our lives. That means that our minds are to be progressively renewed by the Word of God and the power of the Spirit so that we can *know* what He expects of us. If we embrace the supernatural view of guidance *alone* as being God's way of guiding his children, we will see little need for developing our minds. All that will matter is that we have heard directly from God. Yet, when we understand how God entrusts to us the great responsibility of knowing His will through the normal processes of our minds, we suddenly realize that developing our mental capacities to the fullest is an absolute necessity! We then will do all in our power to keep our minds renewed since it directly affects our ability to comprehend God's will.

Horses and Mules

Along with Romans 12:1-2, another portion of Scripture, this time taken from the Old Testament, will help us to understand the relationship between the renewed mind and divine guidance. Psalm 32, written by David centuries before the apostle Paul penned his letter to the Romans, powerfully confirms the apostle's teaching regarding the place of the renewed mind in discovering the will of God.

Like Psalm 51, this Psalm was written by David after he committed adultery with Bathsheba and arranged for the murder of her husband. In the first half of the Psalm, he describes his mental and emotional state prior to being exposed by Nathan (see II Samuel 12). He describes feeling like a runner on a hot summer day, totally depleted of all strength and vitality (32:4). Yet after confessing his sin and receiving that amazing grace by which He was fully pardoned, he came alive again! Recalling that under the Law of Moses there was no sacrifice for adultery or murder, it is clear that David experienced nothing less than New Covenant mercies even while living under the old covenant. This was a foretaste of what his Greater Son would one day make available for all the children of God.

In the second part of the Psalm (verses 8-11) David shifts the focus from his experience of forgiveness to God's promise to guide him in all of his affairs ("I will instruct you and teach you in the way you should go, I will counsel you and watch over you"). Specifically, God says that he would "guide him with his eye" (32:8b, King James Version). Many believe this refers to the manner by which Eastern kings communicated their desires to their servants which stood around the throne. Those servants were so intimately acquainted with their masters, they discerned even in the slightest eye movements their most intimate desires. In the same way, God promises such intimacy with David that he will be able to discern the very intimations of His heart. Talk about being guided by God!

Yet such exquisite guidance is promised on the assumption that David exercise his mind to the fullest: "Do not be like the horse or the mule *which have no understanding* but must be controlled by bit and bridle or they will not come to you" (32:9, italics mine). David should not expect that God will guide him in the same way farmers guide farm animals—with bit and bridle in order to get them to obey. Farm animals require these things precisely because they have rudimentary brains, and therefore are without *understanding* (32:9). Humans, on the other hand, *do* have understanding and are expected to use it when it comes to discerning what God wants.

Considering the marvelous way God promises to guide us through the fullest use of our minds, we stand in awe. God has purposed that so much rest on our sanctified minds! No wonder Paul impels believers to be "transformed by the *renewing* of their minds." Only by developing our minds to the fullest can we expect to discern His good and perfect will for our lives.

Trivializing the Gospel

Mindlessness has taken its toll on another important area of Christian living, *evangelism*. If there is any area where clear thinking is essential, it is when we are engaged in the holy act of bringing the good news to the lost. Sadly, there is almost no area where mindlessness has been more evident. In our attempts to win others to the faith, many well-intentioned believers have greatly dishonored the Name they sought to uphold. Mindless evangelism has not helped the cause of Christ.

Why is so much modern evangelism associated with mindlessness? In part, it is due to what I mentioned earlier in this chapter—our obsession with keeping the Gospel simple when offering it to others. In itself, this desire to keep the message simple is a good thing. It is rooted in a desire to be like the Lord Himself, Who was the master of taking profound mysteries and making them simple so that a child could grasp them. His parables are the ultimate example of that. They take the complex realities of the kingdom of God and explain them in such a way, anyone can grasp their significance.

So at face value, this desire to not complicate the Gospel when sharing it is certainly commendable. The problem though, is that we sometimes fail to distinguish between the desire to keep it simple, and the temptation to trivialize it. The two are not the same, and failure to recognize this has had disastrous results for the Gospel. According to the dictionary, to trivialize something is to "make something seem less important, significant, or complex than it really is." How do we trivialize the Gospel? When we handle it in such a way as to give the impression that it is not really important, the world doesn't bother take it seriously. Why would people bother to take it seriously when it is presented with the same seriousness as a television commercial or ad campaign?

Several years ago, Christians posted the phrase "I Found It" on automobiles and billboards, in the hope that people's curiosity would be aroused and they would ask them what they had found. Now I have no doubt that there were some whose curiosity was piqued by this campaign. Nevertheless in the long run, I believe this campaign hindered rather than furthered the cause of the Gospel. When we succumb to the temptation to reduce the Gospel to quaint phrases, we unknowingly trivialize it. I am convinced that many people reject the Gospel today, not because they believe it to be untrue but because they find it inadequate to deal with the complexities of modern life. When we trivialize it, we only give credence to the idea that the Gospel is inadequate. When people hear quaint phrases and slick slogans instead of well convincing arguments for the Gospel, they conclude that it must not be important, since those defending it have not bothered to think very deeply about it.

Another way we can unknowingly trivialize the message is by leaning too heavily on personal testimony when sharing it. Now it is certainly appropriate at times to use personal testimony when attempting to convince others of the truth of the Gospel. At least on two occasions the apostle Paul told the personal story of his conversion while defending the Gospel (Acts 22:1-21, 26:9-18). Still, the record of the book of Acts makes it clear that he did not rely upon personal testimony as the primary means of communicating the message. Luke uses the word reasoned to describe Paul's work in the synagogue as well as when he debated the Greek philosophers of his day (Acts 17:2, 17). That word is derived from the Greek word dialegomai which the lexicon defines as "thinking different things with one's self, mingling thought with thought, pondering, revolving in mind." (Acts 17:17 NAS). When applied to the apostle it means that he relied on reasonable and rational arguments in his defense of the Gospel and not merely personal testimony. So should we when sharing the faith with others.

We learn from Paul's example that true evangelistic preaching is always first aimed at convincing the mind. That means that evangelism is theological in nature. The goal of evangelistic preaching is to provide sinners with a rational understanding of such things as the nature of God, the person of Jesus Christ, His redemptive work, and its application to our lives. The Holy Spirit then uses these rational and reasonable arguments to convince people of the truth of the Gospel. In the first century, the Church was effective precisely because it presented well-reasoned arguments for the Gospel. In fact, it was the intellectual quality of the early Christians that made the faith so appealing to others as D.M. Baillie points out:

> "Dr. T.R. Glover, who was such an authority on that period (the early centuries A.D.), tells us that one reason why Christianity conquered the

world was because it did better thinking than the rest of the world. It not only knew better how to live and how to die; it also knew how to think. It "out-thought" the world. Here is a deeply interesting passage: 'The Christian read the best books, assimilated them, and lived the freest intellectual life the world had. Jesus had set him free to be true to fact. There is no place for an ignorant Christian. From the very start every Christian had to know and to understand, and he had to read the Gospels, he had to be able to give a reason for his faith. They read about Jesus, and they knew him, and they where they stood… Who did the thinking in that ancient world? Again and again it was the Christian. He out-thought the world (D. M. Baillie, *To Whom Shall We Go*, Scribner, pgs. 62-63).

Always Ready To Make a Defense

In this first epistle the apostle Peter instructs believers to "always be prepared to give an answer" when asked to give a reason for their faith (I Peter 3:15). Peter assumes that as believers live before others they will be asked to explain *why* they hold to their Christian beliefs. All such inquiries believers must be ready to answer. The word *answer* in this passage is the translation of the Greek word *apologia* from which our English word *apology* is derived. From this word (apologia) the whole area of study known as *Apologetics*—the science of defending the Gospel through reasonable and rational arguments—is derived. In modern English, an *apology* carries negative connotations; you have done something wrong and you must issue an apology. But in the ancient world an *apology* was a defense of a position that was being assailed by an opponent, such as when a lawyer defended a client who was being accused in a court of law. Understood in this sense, Peter is exhorting believers to be well-equipped to defend the Gospel when they stand on trial before the bar of the world.

Sadly, few believers today are prepared to defend the Gospel in this manner. Most rely on personal testimony, being ill-equipped to defend the message with well-reasoned arguments. What is desperately needed today is the emergence of a new generation of believers who have thought deeply about the faith so that they can adequately defend it before an unbelieving world. They will first have to abandon unscriptural ideas regarding the mind if they want to be equipped to defend the truth before a truth-starved world.

Summing It Up

In the previous chapter, we saw how God created us with a wonderful capacity to reason so as to understand both our Creator and the universe He created. It is this capacity more than anything else which separates us from the rest of the created order. In this chapter, we focused on the mind as the critical organ in Christian discipleship as well. If we want to be fruitful disciples we cannot ignore the cultivation of our minds. To treat our intellects with contempt not only is a negation of our humanity, it shortchanges our ability to live effective Christian lives in this world.

It is not easy for a person to admit that they have spent the majority of their Christian life neglecting this most important part of Christian development. Those willing to admit, however, will be richly rewarded. Coming alive intellectually is a sure way of supercharging a Christian life which was previously boring. In the next chapter, I explore more fully the reason for much of the boredom in the house of God today and recommend as its cure something that, at first glance, might seem like the *reason* for much of our boredom rather than its cure. Nevertheless, it is a tried and true antidote for boredom in the Christian life, and a solution desperately needed today if we are once again to rekindle a passion for truth in the house of God.

CHAPTER SIX

The Cure for Boredom with God

Looking around the Church today, one gets the impression that many believers are bored with God. I don't mean that they show no interest in Christian activities such as church going, or involvement in Christian service. People continue to attend worship services and engage in Christian service. What I am referring to is the fact that the average churchgoer today exhibits very little hunger *for* God Himself. Few seem mesmerized by the majesty and grandeur of the God of Scripture.

There are a number of ways we can gauge the level of boredom in the Church today. Take the state of worship for example. It is not uncommon today for worship leaders to feel the need to manipulate people in order to get them to worship. The fact that they feel the need to do this at all is evidence that people are bored with God; if they weren't, such tactics would be unnecessary and people would freely abandon themselves to God in worship. Instead, they have to be cajoled and prodded to offer Him worship.

Another area where boredom is evident in many churches today is the lack of desire to sit under sound, biblical teaching. To placate their congregations many pastors no longer regularly present the God of Scripture in all his glory in their sermons. Instead, they have resorted instead to *self-help* sermons—ten principles for a better life, five steps to spiritual maturity, ten principles for a better marriage. Consequently, many in this generation are strangers to the kind of preaching and teaching that sustained past generations, preaching which focused on presenting the God of Scripture to people so that the full weight of His glory was known. Such preaching was not aimed at making the worshipper feel better about himself, but bringing him face to face with the God of glory.

Why is there such boredom with God and His word in the Church today? The truth is, it is not the God of the Bible they are bored with, but the boring god of Christendom. Far from inspiring dread and awe, this god is quite predictable (and manageable) requiring little more than attendance at a few church services and a buck in an offering plate. No wonder people are bored. They are no longer worshipping the glorious God of Scripture, but rather a sad caricature of Him.

The truth is, it is impossible to know the God of Scripture and be bored with Him. Simply put, He is the most exciting Person in the universe! Those privileged to stand in His presence and behold Him are thrilled to the very core of their beings. The Bible exhausts the vernacular in describing what He is like—holy, happy, majestic, awe-inspiring, unapproachable, unknowable, without fault, above all, in all, through all. The notion, therefore, that a person could be bored with such a Being is utterly blasphemous.

If we are bored, it is not with God Himself, but with a god that we have invented who is a distortion of the true God of the Bible. Yet thankfully there is a cure for this boredom. If our boredom is the result of our having traded the God of Scripture for the boring god of Christendom, the remedy is to repent and turn back again to the living God. But first, we will need to gain a proper knowledge of Him, and that can only come by ransacking the Scriptures until the full knowledge of Him is before us. This is infinitely more than merely reading the Bible (though we must do that) but seeking in its pages to understand who God is. In a word, the cure for our boredom is *theology*!

The previous statement was not a misprint. I wholeheartedly believe that theology is God's means of curing us from our boredom. Since our boredom was caused by a failure to seriously apprehend the God of Scripture, it stands to reason that it is only by thoroughly studying our Bibles until we really discover what God is like that we will find a cure for our boredom. That what is that *theology* essentially is. It is the knowledge of God gained through diligently searching the pages of Scripture until we come face to face with Him and what He has done in the work of his lovely Son.

Other cures for boredom abound on the market today. Most of them offer quick fixes, such as dynamic spiritual experiences and attendance at exciting meetings. But these cannot permanently cure our boredom. What is needed is nothing less than a total change in our concept of God. This is no quick fix but a proven method requiring a lifetime of searching the Scriptures, which is probably why it's not popular. Since our boredom with God is rooted in a lack of mental stimulation (a failure to think deeply about the God revealed in Scripture), the only cure is to awaken our minds to deeply engage Scripture until He is fully known.

Loving God With Our Minds

The Synoptic Gospels (Matthew, Mark, Luke) record how that during Passion Week various Jewish leaders questioned the Lord Jesus in order to trap Him in something He said (Matthew 21, Mark 12, Luke 20). These leaders included a certain scribe who asked Him a question regarding which commandment was the greatest (Mark 12:28). That question was being hotly debated among the various schools of Judaism in Jesus' day. Judaism had reduced the Law to (only) 613 commandments and the various rabbinic schools at the time vigorously argued about which of these was the greatest. So this scribe was asking Jesus to weigh in on the debate, most likely in the hope that He would discredit Himself with some of the branches of

Judaism. Our Lord answered him by quoting from the sixth chapter of Deuteronomy: *"Love the Lord your God with all your heart and with all your soul and with all your mind"* (Deuteronomy 6:5, Matthew 22:37). These words follow the traditional *Shema*, the technical term for Deuteronomy 6:4 considered by Jews to be the holiest verse in the Hebrew Bible. In answering the scribe with this verse our Lord was teaching that no commandment exceeded that of *loving* God with all one's faculties. Loving one's neighbor as himself was the natural outgrowth of the first. As far as Jesus was concerned, the entire Law and Prophets hung on these two commandments.

Included in this commandment to love God with all of our faculties is the call to love God with our minds. Sadly, many believers today have ignored that aspect of loving God. For them, loving God is largely a matter of cultivating certain feelings rather than awakening their minds to fully apprehend who God is. It is rare today to find churches where the members are challenged to think deeply as a vital component of their love for God. As I stated in the previous chapter, in my early years as a disciple I cannot recall hearing even one sermon which exhorted us to realize the importance of the mind in our devotion to Christ. I heard a multitude of messages on the need to 'feel God's presence' or 'make a decision for Jesus' but relatively nothing about the need to offer God my mind. No wonder I concluded that loving God had little to do with the mind and was largely about cultivating certain feelings.

One of the reasons that many believers ignore the mind in their devotion to Christ is that they (mistakenly) believe that a deep gulf exists between the heart and the mind. But this is largely a Western invention. When the Bible refers to the *heart* it means our whole inner life which includes the mind. To separate them (as many Westerners do) is to commit a fundamental error. Author Os Guiness comments on this:

> "Never mind that 'heart' in the Bible is more a matter of understanding than sentiment—so 'heart' versus 'head' is a false choice. Never

mind that the Spirit of truth is also the Spirit of love and power—so truth must never be pitted against love and power. Ever since the mid-eighteenth century we evangelicals have had a natural bias towards the Tin Woodman's choice—empty brains and happy hearts. We even glory in our choice" (*Fit Bodies, Fat Minds*, Os Guinness, page 31).

While Moses in the passage in Deuteronomy (6:5) separates each human faculty (heart, soul, mind, strength) in real life they cannot be separated. Moses is simply teaching the Israelites that their entire *inner* being must be involved in their devotion to God. The notion therefore that our hearts can grow in love for God *apart* from our minds is wholly unscriptural. God has designed for us to love Hims with all of our inner and outer faculties. A major part of that devotion is to learn to love Him with our mind. When I discovered, as a young believer, the place the mind must hold in my devotion to God, a whole new world opened up! I soon discovered that developing my mind to its fullest capacity was actually part of that "acceptable worship" the apostle Paul spoke of in Romans (Romans 12:2). Far from leading me away from loving God, true devotion to God demanded the fullest development of my mind:

> "Loving God with our minds is not finally a question of orthodoxy, but of love. Offering up our minds to God in all our thinking is part of our praise. Anti-intellectualism is quite simply a sin. Evangelicals must address it as such, beyond all excuses, evasions, or rationalization of false piety" (ibid, page 18).

Why then does the notion that we must choose between 'head and heart' in the development of Christian spirituality remain so popular today? It is largely the result of the emergence of *Pietism* and its influence in the Church. Os Guinness defines Pietism as "a heart religion, which places piety, or total life devotion, at the center of the Christian faith" (Ibid, page 34). Understood in this way, Pietism is not so much a movement as it is an idea about Christian spirituality. What could possibly be wrong with an emphasis on total devotion to God? Nothing; except that most pietists devalue the place of the mind when it comes to living the Christian life. Picking up many many pietistic devotional books on the market today one often finds the oft repeated theme that we must choose between "well-developed minds with little passion for God" or "little intellectual development with hearts brimming with love for God." Yet, as we have seen, such a choice is bogus. God intends for us to enjoy a rich emotional life even while developing our intellects to the fullest. In fact, this is the true way of achieving biblical spirituality.

How do we train our minds to love God? One important way is by *meditating* upon the Scriptures until the full impact of the revelation of God is felt. This is *Christian* meditation and it differs greatly from other forms of meditation such as those practiced in the East. Those Eastern forms, for the most part, require their adherents to *empty* their minds in order to achieve a state of oneness or bliss. Christian meditation, on the other hand, never directs us to empty our minds but to *focus* them on the Word of God. The Hebrew word for *meditate* implies the rolling of something over again and again in the mind until it is easily retained. It has often been compared to a cow chewing its cud—the cow regurgitates its food chewing it again and again until it is fully masticated. In the same way, meditating upon Scripture means that we are constantly rolling it around in our minds until it becomes a real part of our inner life.

The loss of this discipline in the Church today has not only meant the loss of the blessings associated with meditation, but a general dulling of the Christian mind as well. To counter this trend we must train a new generation of believers to love God through vigorous intellectual exercise. They must be taught that God is glorified as much by the proper exercise of the mind as He is by fervent prayer. The result will not only be that God is glorified, but that God's people also gain a greater effectiveness in sharing the Gospel as well.

Theology: God's Answer to Boredom

I mentioned at the beginning of this chapter that the study of theology is a major means of preventing boredom in the Christian life.

I am convinced that training our minds to relish all Scripture reveals about our glorious God will move us from spiritual boredom to a life of true spiritual fulfillment. Why do many people equate theology with boredom? The most important reason is that they have improper ideas about what theology is. The word 'theology' for many people drums up the idea of irrelevant information about God that only quasi-scholars and intellectuals can understand. So it is not surprising that theology is equated with boredom. Thankfully though, that is not what theology is. It is not irrelevant information about God that only intellectuals can understand, but the study of God and His glorious plan for His creatures as revealed in Holy Scripture. How could such a study ever be boring? Allowing the full weight of what God says about Himself and His plan for His creatures to weigh upon our minds is the most exciting venture we can pursue.

The truth is, many are bored in the church today, not because they have studied theology and found it to be boring, but because they are 'brain-starved.' They have been living a Christian life which satisfies their emotions while leaving their minds severely malnourished. They are like a person who has lived the entirety of his life on a diet consisting primarily of cotton candy. Initially, the taste of cotton candy is wonderful and the person can't seem to get enough of it. Yet, before long, that person will develop certain physical deficiencies because of a lack of proper nutrients. In the same way, Christians who live the entirety of their spiritual lives on emotions and spiritual experiences with little concern for the development of their minds will eventually manifest certain spiritual deficiencies as well. They may enjoy rich emotional experiences, yet unless they learn to exercise their minds to the fullest, they will remain spiritually shallow.

The only remedy for such shallowness is *theology*—a deep penetrating study of Scripture which brings us face to face with the person of God. Such theological study is a sure cure for the boredom many saints experience today. We should not fear that studying theology will make us lazy and unfruitful in our Christian lives. While it is true that many study theology in order to impress others with their knowledge, those studying it in order to deepen their personal knowledge of God will find a rich harvest for the soul.

I am living proof that theology leads to great spiritual richness. It has been through theological study that the person of God has become more and more real to me. Far from making me idle, the study of theology has actually energized my Christian service. This should not be surprising. As God is progressively revealed to our minds, this creates a desire to give ourselves more fully to Him. There have been times during my theological studies when the greatness of God made such an impression upon my soul I had to put down the book I was reading and fall on my face to worship God! Through theological study my heart and head have grown at the same time.

Various Branches of Theology

Once we are convinced that theology is a cure for boredom, how should we go about studying it? The best approach is a *systematic* one. This approach will aid us in becoming more acquainted with the main components of biblical theology. Traditionally, a systematic study of Scripture is one that examines the various branches of biblical theology. In the remainder of this chapter I will briefly describe some of the branches of theological study which are generally viewed as *systematic*. This is in no way meant to be exhaustive, but a simple overview of each of the important areas we will need to become acquainted in our quest for a biblical theology.

The various branches of biblical theology deal with such things as the *nature of God*, (theology), the *nature of Holy Scripture*, the *nature of man* (anthropology), the *nature of Christ* (Christology), the nature of our *divine salvation* (soteriology), and the nature of the Person and work of the Holy Spirit (pneumatology). We would add to that the study of 'last things' commonly known as *eschatology*. Each one is important in setting forth a well-balanced statement of biblical faith. By properly understanding each we will be saved from a life of (mental) boredom. Within the branches themselves are more precise categories, but these serve as the major components of a biblical theology. A brief description of each follows.

The Nature of God (Theology)

The first branch of theology and by far the most important is the study of the *nature* and *attributes* of God as revealed in Scripture. The Bible is not a book primarily about the end times or angels or even salvation, but a book about *God*. If we come to the Bible in order to find God, we will discover riches beyond our wildest dreams. All who would know God must study the Scriptures in order to find Him. That is not to say that the act of reading the Bible *alone* guarantees that we will gain knowledge of God. The knowledge gained from Scripture must be coupled with personal experience in order to form an adequate knowledge of God. Nevertheless, if we are serious about knowing Him we will acquaint ourselves with Holy Scripture, for it contains a revelation of the God Who has saved us.

The first thing which strikes us about God as He is presented in Scripture is that He is absolutely unique—there is simply no one else like Him in the entire universe! Scripture reveals that He is 'self-existent,' a theological term meaning He owes his existence to no one else since He has always existed. I once tried to explain this aspect of God's being to my two youngest sons. They had no difficulty understanding how God's being will never end since as eternal beings they also share this quality. Yet when it came to my explaining to them how God also had *no* beginning, their little minds couldn't fathom it. And for that matter, neither could mine. That's because it is impossible for finite beings to come to terms with a being who never *wasn't*! When I exercise my mind to try to grasp it I can only join David in uttering, "Such knowledge is too wonderful for me, too lofty for me to attain" (Psalm 139:6).

Systematic theology is the study of each of these wonderful attributes of God such as His sovereignty, holiness, justice, love, mercy, power, etc. Together, they present us with the Scriptural portrait of the God with whom we have to do. Dr. Robert L. Reymond sums up what we can expect from a study of theology:

> "The acquisition of a systematic theology of the doctrine of God that will pass the muster of Scripture is surely one of the most demanding intellectual enterprises man will ever undertake. The 'vast deeps' of the Ultimate Subject of theology, who is 'infinite, eternal, and unchangeable, in His being, wisdom, power, holiness, justice, goodness and truth' (Westminster Short Catechism, Question 4), will often search the creature's understanding beyond his powers of comprehension and humble him as nothing else can or will" (A New Systematic Theology of the Christian Faith, Dr. Robert Reymond, page 129).

Engaging in a study of the nature of God in Scripture is a sure way to avoid boredom in the Christian life. I have yet to find a person engaged in a serious study of the person of God who would rather be playing a board game or watching a movie. If they were bored, it was not because the subject was boring, but because they had no real relationship with God. Exercising our brains to fully comprehend the revelation of God contained in Scripture is the most wonderful exercise redeemed creatures can engage in. It is the full-time occupation of the angels in heaven and as humans who have been rescued by Christ, it should be ours as well.

The Nature of Scripture

Any serious study of theology will also include a study of God's Word *written*. Throughout the history of the Church, true believers have always held the highest view of Holy Scripture. No greater statement regarding the nature of God's Word has ever been penned than that contained in the Westminster Confession:

"Although the light of nature, and the works of creation and provi-
dence, do so far manifest the goodness, wisdom, and power of God,
as to leave men inexcusable, yet are they not sufficient to give that
knowledge of God, and of His will, which is necessary to salvation;
therefore it pleased the Lord, at sundry times, and in divers manners,
to reveal himself, and to declare that His will into His church; and afterwards for the better preserving and propagating of the truth, and
for the more sure establishment and comfort of the church against
the corruption of the flesh, and the malice of Satan and of the world,
to commit the same wholly unto writing; which the Holy Scripture to
be most necessary; those former ways of God's revealing His will unto
His people being now ceased" (Westminister Confession of Faith, I/i).

This important statement underscores why a written record of
God's Word is necessary by distinguishing between two types of revelation: *general* and *special*. General revelation is what God has made
known about Himself through what He has made; what we can learn
about God from observing such things as the stellar universe, the
earth, and all life forms on it. This type of revelation provides us
with *some* knowledge of God in that we can look at the things that are
made and learn something about the Creator. Yet it is not adequate
for understanding God's plan of salvation for fallen creatures through
Christ. For that, it was necessary that God speak through the *special*
medium of apostles and prophets. And what He spoke was written
down and is now preserved for us in Holy Scripture (Ephesians 2:20).
It exceeds general revelation, in that it contains a revelation of God's
redemptive purpose which could not have been known unless God
had revealed it to us. And since God has taken the initiative to have
His thoughts written down for us in words we can understand, each
person has the unique privilege of hearing God speak to them whenever they read it.

Special revelation is that which God has revealed about His pur-
pose and plan in Christ. How exciting it is to read the very words of
God through which we can understand this wonderful plan in Christ.
If the words of the Bible were simply man's words they might contain

interesting or useful information, but if they are the very words of the living God, studying them in order to hear God speak to us should be the most exciting thing we will ever do.

A quick scan of Church history reveals that the Church has always been the healthiest at those times when it has maintained the highest view of Scripture. Sadly, she has not always done so. Nevertheless, her attitude towards God in any age is generally determined by her attitude towards Holy Scripture.

The Nature of Man (Anthropology)

Another important component of biblical theology is *Anthropology*; the study of human beings created in the image and likeness of God. Since God made us like Himself we are absolutely unique in the created order. Therefore, the study of human beings is an important component of biblical theology. It focuses on both what we were originally created to be, as well as what we have *now* become as creatures who have left their first estate. In biblical terms we are *fallen*—created originally in God's image and likeness, but now radically distorted through the entrance of sin into the race. Any study of human beings therefore must take into account this twofold aspect of humanity. Here, I will address our uniqueness as created beings, leaving the matter of our sinfulness for the section which follows.

The first two chapters of Genesis instruct us as to the unique place God gave humans in the created order. Prior to the creation of Adam, animals held the highest place in God's world. Yet when Adam appeared, that place was given to humans. This is borne out by the fact that only to Adam was given the task of naming the animals. This undoubtedly involved more than merely attaching a name to each species, but also required that Adam have a keen awareness of the unique nature of each. By implication, this meant Adam had a superior intellect to those creatures which he was to name. This is why no suitable helpmate could be found for Adam among the animal kingdom but had to be taken from *within* himself (Genesis 2:20). We learn much later in the New Testament that the forming of a bride for Adam in the Garden prefigured the mystery of God in creating an eternal companion for His Son (Ephesians 5:32).

Apart from the biblical record, we would have no way of understanding our uniqueness in the divine order. Without the vital teaching of Scripture, we would be justified in concluding that there is little difference between animals and humans. Once we understand the biblical truth of the primacy of human beings, we can understand that there is a vast difference between animals and humans. While that certainly doesn't justify cruel treatment of animals by humans, it does set forth human beings as superior among the creatures which the Lord God has made.

There are several benefits which we may derive from understanding Biblical Anthropology. First, it assists us in our *social* interactions with other human beings. Since the entirety of our lives are lived in relationship to others, knowing how God has made us enhances our ability to relate to others. Whenever I meet another person, I am reminded that he or she is made in the image and likeness of God and therefore I must treat them accordingly. This is the point that James makes in his letter when warning us against slandering others (James 3:9). Only by knowing that people are made in God's own image and likeness can we treat them with the respect due them as wondrous creations of God.

Anthropology also helps us to understand what God expects of us as redeemed creatures. In their zeal for sanctification, many believers tend to despise their own humanity. They often forget that it is not our humanity which is the problem, but rather the fact that we are sinful. God actually celebrates our humanness, as evident by the fact that His Son left heaven and became a *real* Man. A proper view of God therefore will lead us to a proper view of human nature as well.

The Sinfulness of Man (Anthropology)

Biblical Anthropology also must deal with the reality that, though created in the image and likeness of God, we are *sinful*—sold into slavery to sin. The account of the original creation of human beings in Genesis is immediately followed by the sad story of Adam's trespass and through him, the subsequent fall of the entire race (Genesis 3). While human beings still maintain the image and likeness of God, that image is now a *distorted* image. Human beings are now a sad caricature of what they were originally created to be. That doesn't mean that we do not still bear the image of God; we do, except that it is now a *marred* image.

The term theologians often use to describe human sinfulness is *depravity*. I have never really liked this term due to the fact that it conveys the idea that we are all as bad as we could be. In actuality though, that is not what the term means. It simply refers to the reality that every faculty of human life is now infected by sin so that our bodies are now 'instruments of unrighteousness' (Romans 6:13). The doctrine of human depravity addresses the age-old question which has long troubled philosophers, 'Why do human beings continually tend towards evil?' It is only in the Christian religion that a full and complete answer to that question is found.

This doctrine of human sinfulness does not deny the essential goodness of human beings as originally created by God. It acknowledges that glorious truth with the caveat that all original goodness has now been marred by sin. Any genuine biblical anthropology must take this into account. The biblical doctrine of the sinfulness of man teaches that all human beings now share in the guilt and corruption of Adam and Eve. This is not an easy doctrine to accept, especially for Americans who place such a high value on human freedom. Theologian Michael Horton explains:

> "This concept is often hard to swallow—particularly in America, where we are saturated with the democratic ideal of being able to decide for ourselves what party we will join. But we did not decide whether

we would belong to the Adamic party; we were born into it. The same is true, though, in a lot of areas. For instance, when Thomas Jefferson drafted the Declaration of Independence, he spoke for you and me. We were not actually there. We didn't get to help him decide what to write. And yet, this document represents us just the same as if we had been there. We were born American citizens, not British, because of individuals who lived and events that took place long before we came along" (*Putting Amazing Back in Grace*, Michael Horton, page 58).

While this doctrine is critical to biblical theology, its importance has been steadily on the decline in the Western Church due in part to the general acceptance in the culture of the presuppositions of Sigmund Freud. Freud viewed human beings not as guilty sinners in need of atonement, but sad victims in need of pity. Sadly, many modern believers have accepted a mixture of Freud and the Gospel which has resulted in a Gospel shorn of any need for human beings to repent and turn from sin by trusting in Jesus Christ. We should not find it surprising that this false Gospel is so popular; after all, sinful men and women always resist facing up to their true condition. This (refusal to face up to our true condition) is in itself is confirmation of the fact that we are exactly what Scripture says—guilty sinners in need of forgiveness and regeneration.

This doctrine of human sinfulness is essential to a proper understanding of our salvation in Christ. Unless we believe that as members of Adam's race we are sinners condemned to eternal damnation, all this talk about God sending His Son to redeem us is much ado about nothing. Christ came to save sinners; if that is not what we are, Christ died in vain. This doctrine therefore is an important precursor to salvation. To the degree we believe the human race is fallen, to that degree we will seek salvation in Christ.

The loss of this biblical anthropological doctrine in the church today has had a devastating affect on the cause of the Gospel. Since few churches today teach the sinfulness of the race (except in a cursory way) people focus on the *symptoms* of their sinfulness rather than the cause. Much preaching today is directed on helping people deal with things such as loneliness, rejection, fear, physical maladies—all things that are symptoms of our real problem. Not surprisingly, few in our churches today are learning to struggle daily against sin. How could they when they have been to focus on the "fruit" of their sinfulness rather than "root" which caused it.

The Nature of Christ (Christology)

Another important branch of biblical theology is *Christology*, the study of our Savior, the Lord Jesus Christ. Author Peter Lewis tells why this is a separate branch of theology:

> "For almost twenty centuries the church has placed one historic figure where it has placed no other man. It has taken the carpenter from first-century Nazareth, Jesus, and ranged Him on the side of deity; making His teaching the absolute authority in our knowledge of God. Jesus' work has become the ground of our salvation, and His person the object of our faith and worship. And church members, drawn from 'every tribe and language and people and nation' (Revelation 5:9), have known Him and served Him, loved Him and hymned Him, preached Him and praised Him" (*The Glory of Christ*, Peter Lewis, page 13).

It is the uniqueness of Jesus which serves as the basis for this aspect of theology. As far as the church is concerned, there is no one like Jesus of Nazareth. That is why the universal church has held him in such high esteem:

> "Jesus occupies a unique place in the mind and heart of the Church because Jesus insisted on that unique place. The church has made many claims for the carpenter from Nazareth, but none higher than He made Himself. The church has not been extravagant in its devotion to Him; it has only been loyal and faithful in responding to the devotion He claimed and still claims" (ibid, page 13).

Even though the New Testament is clear on the central place this Person occupies in the divine economy, the church has not had an easy time coming to terms with Him. Many of the New Testament letters were written to churches which had been inundated with heresies which distorted the Person and work of Christ. Throughout the two thousand year history of the church various church councils were convened to uphold the deity of Christ when it was under attack from the heretics. In some ways we should be thankful for these enemies of the faith, for they brought to the forefront some of the greatest thinkers the Church has ever known. Men like Augustine, Tertullian, and the Cappadocian Fathers used their incredible intellectual powers (as well as their love for Christ) to defend the faith. In the process, they gave the church some of its greatest theology regarding the Person and work of the Lord Jesus Christ.

Several years ago, I was invited to teach a course in Church History at a divinity college. As I was preparing for my lectures on the early Christian centuries, I read about many of the lively debates among the church Fathers over the relationship between the humanity and deity of the Lord Jesus Christ. At first I was critical of these men who seemed so willing to split hairs over the most minute aspects of Christ's nature. Yet the more I studied their writings, the more I realized that these very debates themselves confirmed that Jesus was exactly who He claimed to be! As far as I can tell there has never been debates in Islam over the person of Mohammed or in Buddhism over Buddha or in Judaism over Moses. While there are debates about how to practice the various religions they founded or what certain teachings within their respective religions mean, that is entirely different from the debates in the early centuries of Christianity. They were were not so much about how to practice Christianity or what certain teachings might mean, but centered in answering the question, *Who* really is this Man, Jesus of Nazareth?

Only a biblical Christology will keep us from a boring Christian life. Both Old and New Testaments heap every superlative imaginable upon Him; language itself is strained to describe this mighty Christ. My personal favorite is in Isaiah chapter nine; "And He will be called *wonderful* Counselor" (Isaiah 9:6). The Hebrew word translated *wonderful* in the text literally means "a wonder," and is used elsewhere of

God's acts of judgment and redemption. Simply stated, Jesus is God's wonder! That means that the Christian life should be a never-ending exploration of God's wonder; Jesus of Nazareth.

There were periods throughout church History in which believers held views of Christ that were utterly beneath Him. In some ways, I think we are living in such a time today. The Jesus often presented in the modern Church is a serious distortion of the New Testament portrait of Him. Dr. R. C. Sproul once referred to the way many churches view Christ as a "cosmic Mr. Rogers." I sometimes refer to Him as the "churchy" Jesus; benign, passive, weak, totally incapable of wrath. This is a far cry from the biblical portrait of the Christ Who overturned the tables of the moneychangers in the temple and who will return one day to judge all men. In his book *Wild at Heart* author John Eldridge captures His true essence:

> "Jesus is no "capon priest," no pale-faced altar boy with his hair parted in the middle, speaking softly, avoiding confrontation, who at last gets himself killed because he has no way out. He works with wood, commands the loyalty of dockworkers. He is the Lord of hosts, the captain of angel armies. And when Christ returns, he is at the head of a dreadful company, mounted on a white horse, with a double-edged sword, his robe dipped in blood (Revelation 19). Now that sounds a lot more like William Wallace than it does Mother Teresa" (*Wild at Heart*, John Eldridge, page 29).

If we want a healthy and robust Christianity we must recapture this biblical portrait of Jesus of Nazareth. That's why Christology is such an important component of biblical theology. It is imperative that the Christ we are coming to know is the biblical Christ and not the boring Christ of Christendom.

The Nature of Salvation (Soteriology)

The final branch of theology is *soteriology:* the study of our glorious salvation in Christ. This also is an important component of biblical theology. It is the study of what God accomplished in redeeming and saving a people for his Name. Gaining a proper understanding of God's work in His Son to secure our salvation is also an essential component of theology.

It is in the book of Romans that we find the most exhaustive teaching in Scripture regarding our divine salvation. The closest thing Paul ever wrote to a book, Romans logically unfolds the nature of Christian salvation from the fall of the race to God's redemption through the death of His Son. The theme of Romans might best be described by the words of the Psalmist: "Salvation is of the Lord" (Psalm 3:8). We learn in Romans that we can take no credit for our salvation, it being totally wrought by the Lord Himself. While the majority of churches today parrot this in their creeds, the reality is often sorely lacking. Many believers act like salvation is a shared effort between themselves and God. God did His part by sending His Son and we must now do our part by accepting Jesus and working hard to prove we're worthy. In Scripture, though, we find no such arrangement. The Bible teaches that salvation is a work of God both in its initiation as well as its completion.

The New Testament teaches us that our salvation is a real salvation holding forth hope both for the present life as well as the life to come. A major aspect of our salvation will only be revealed at the appearing of our Lord (I Peter 1:5). Yet those who are in Christ now are *really* saved from the penalty of their sins and presently share in the life of Christ (Romans 5:10). The evidence that we are in Christ is that God has given us the Spirit in our hearts (Romans 8:9). And because the Spirit indwells us, we are being progressively sanctified while we await full salvation when the Lord of glory appears. The phrase often used to convey this is 'already, but not yet'—the believer *already* has salvation in Christ but is not *yet* in full possession of it. The full manifestation of salvation will only be known when the Lord Jesus appears at which time He will transform our lowly bodies into a body like His own (I John 3:1-2).

A good understanding of salvation will also keep our Christian lives from falling into the doldrums. Realizing the extent to which God has gone to rescue us from both the penalty and power of sin is cause for wonder. That is why the apostle Paul, at the close of the doctrinal section of Romans where he has fully explained our divine salvation (Romans 1-11), breaks out into a doxology extolling God for his glorious wisdom and insight (Romans 11:33-36). The same things appear in the first chapter of Ephesians where, in words which defy language, Paul extols each member of the blessed Trinity for their contribution to our glorious salvation (Ephesians 1:3-14). We can only praise God for His glorious plan to save us which was put into effect by the coming of Christ and made real in us by the presence of the Holy Spirit.

The Nature of the Holy Spirit (Pneumatology)

Another important branch of theology we must study is that of Pneumatology: the study of the Person and work of the Holy Spirit, the blessed third Person of the Godhead. This branch of theology focuses on the Holy Spirit as a Person rather than an impersonal force. In the work of salvation, the Holy Spirit takes all that was accomplished by the Son through his death and resurrection and applies it to the sinner so that he or she is brought to life. Without the work of the Spirit, all that the Son achieved at Calvary and by the resurrection would have no application to our lives.

In theology, the study of the Holy Spirit is often sorely neglected. The Puritan John Owen wrote a brilliant work entitled *Pneumatology* in which he posited the idea that the Holy Spirit and his work was the central emphasis of the Reformation. Without this emphasis, it is possible to educate our brains while not partaking of real spiritual life.

To Sum It Up

With such a rich theological heritage how could we ever be bored? A true understanding of who God is, as well as what He has done on our behalf, will definitely save us from passionless religion. We must never forget that the pathway to the heart is always and ever *through* the mind. It is through the study of theology therefore that our hearts and minds are greatly enlarged and we are drawn to seek after a true knowledge of our God and Savior.

We should never fear that studying theology will cause us to be devoid of passion for God Himself. While there will always be those who study God merely to gain theoretical knowledge rather than cultivate a true knowledge of God, this need not be our lot. As we learn to meditate deeply on God Himself as revealed in Scripture, we will discover that as our mind is enlarged, our passion for God increases as well. That is why some of the greatest thinkers the Church has known were men and women of rich emotional experiences in God as well. In the next chapter, we examine more fully how the development of the life of the mind is the safest way of guaranteeing rich emotional enjoyment in God. To Him be the glory!

CHAPTER SEVEN

Enjoying God
(Without Losing Your Mind)

His name was Jonathan Edwards. He lived in pre-Colonial America at the time when the foundation of our own nation was being laid. He never owned a computer or a typewriter. He lived before many of the breakthroughs in modern medicine were discovered. In his day the average life span of a man was about twenty-six. For most of his life he struggled with a debilitating disease for which he had none of the medicines which have made life manageable for so many today. As a result, he lived in constant pain. Yet he learned to bear it.

During his lifetime, Edwards produced a massive amount of literature, all written painstakingly by his own hand. Due to poor eyesight he wrote by candlelight, hunched over his paper for hours a day. Considering his circumstances, the volume of literature he produced is staggering. He wrote not only about religious topics, but areas of scientific inquiry and philosophy as well. His writings reveal the depth of his mind. To this day, he is considered by many to be one of America's premiere thinkers.

Edwards inherited the pastorate of a New England congregation from his grandfather who had been pastor for many years. Even by the standards of his own day, he was anything but a typical pastor. Believing that the most important thing he could do to care for his people was to develop his own spiritual life, he spent an average of twelve to thirteen hours a day in his office praying, studying, and compiling his writings. While members of his congregation were free to call on him if any had need, Edwards rarely visited his flock. It wasn't because he didn't care for those entrusted to him, but due to his strong conviction that he could not give his people what he himself did not possess. So he chose to spend the majority of his time alone with God, thoroughly convinced that by so doing, his flock would be the beneficiaries of the knowledge of God he gained.

Edwards' favorite pastime was the study of theology. He read deep theological books requiring the fullest exercise of his intellectual powers. For Edwards, the knowledge of God was the most precious thing on earth and he made it his aim to master the basic components of biblical theology. That he is considered to be one of America's premiere theologians is amazing, when considering the meager resources available to him at the time. Yet Edwards knew that it was not the number of books one read but how deeply they were mined that mattered most. Not surprisingly, Edwards' sermons were packed with theology drawn from his deep theological studies.

You might assume that sermons so rich in theological content would be boring, yet nothing could be further from the truth. Jonathan Edwards is considered to be one of the greatest preachers ever to grace the American continent! In his day, the whole of New England was swept up in revival fire, and Edwards' preaching was at the center of it. He preached a famous sermon during that period entitled *Sinners in the Hands of an Angry God.* When Edwards read the sermon in the church it produced such conviction of sin, many of the people held on to the pews as the reality of the terrors of hell were being presented to them.

Did you catch the previous statement—that Edwards *read* his sermon? While scholars debate whether he read all of his sermons, it is clear that he did read some of them. And he did so with very little attempt at moving people emotionally:

"From the testimonies of his contemporaries we know that Edward's sermons were tremendously powerful in their effect on the people in his Northampton congregation. It was not because he was anything like the dramatic orator that George Whitfield was. In the days of the awakening he still wrote his sermons out in full and read them with few gestures" (*The Supremacy of God in Preaching*, John Piper, pp. 49)

Can you imagine someone reading a sermon in a church today? Most of us are so accustomed to preaching that moves our emotions we could not possibly fathom the idea of a pre-Colonial man reading a sermon to his congregation. Yet as the Spirit took the truth in Edwards' sermons and applied it to the hearers, it produced deep conviction of sin. Though not an evangelist like George Whitfield, hundreds were swept into the kingdom through his ministry. Edwards demonstrated the fact that truth enlivened by the power of the Spirit has life-changing power, even when uttered without the typical emotional antics that have come to characterize so much modern preaching.

Edwards was eventually driven from his congregation at Northampton and spent the majority of his remaining years ministering to the American Indians under the most horrid conditions. Afterwards, he became president of Yale for a short while before his death. Though remaining an obscure pastor for many years in a small New England town, he is forever known as one of the most important figures attached to American Christianity. Both followers and critics alike agree that Jonathan Edwards possessed one of the most brilliant minds ever to grace the American Continent.

Jonathan Edwards: Great Thinking to the Glory of God

I previously mentioned the volume of literature Jonathan Edwards produced during his lifetime. If not for his voluminous writings he would not be well known today. Even with all of the modern conveniences we enjoy today, it would be difficult to produce the same amount of work in one lifetime. Besides his theological volumes, he filled his journals with thousands of observations culled from the

musings of his mind on the various topics he entertained. So broad
was Edwards' mind that even those not sympathetic to the Christian
Gospel have come to admire it:

> "Never was a triumph of genius more decisive than that of Jonathan
> Edwards. By the concurrent voice of all who have perused his writ-
> ings, he is assigned one of the first, if not the very first place, amongst
> the masters of human reason. Many of the most acute metaphysicians
> and accomplished divines of the past and present age, have been the
> most ardent of his admirers; we refer to such men as Hume, Mack-
> intosh, Stewart, Robert Hall, and Chalmers. All these celebrated men
> differed from Edwards in some of his most cherished speculations, and
> some of them abhorred all the peculiar doctrines, on the explication
> and defense of which he concentrated the full force of his mighty in-
> tellect; yet they all agree in the homage they render to that intellect;
> like that of a few other very great minds, it was too powerful to allow
> even the proverbial meanness of controversial animosity to attempt
> the ungracious work of depreciation" (*The Works of Jonathan Edwards,
> An Essay on the Genius and Writings of Jonathan Edwards*, pp. i)

One might suppose that with such a focus on developing his mind
Edwards was a passionless intellectual who shunned all emotion in his
spiritual life. In reality, Jonathan Edwards is considered to be one of
the most passionate men the Christian ministry has ever produced! His
journals abound with accounts of the depth of his feeling for God. He
was no passionless theologian but a white-hot man of God who spent
most of his time ardently pursuing the God of his salvation. For Edwards, the rational and emotional realms were intimately connected,
which is why he cultivated his mind to the fullest. He firmly believed
that by so doing he would increase his experience of God as well.

Edwards would stand at odds with many today who believe that
strenuous thinking is actually a hindrance to feeling. On the contrary;
Edwards taught that the way to enlarge one's affections was by enlarg-
ing the mind. He did not believe that there was a dichotomy between
the development of the mind and increased passion for God. For Edwards, one quite naturally led to the other.

The Puritans: Brilliant Minds and Passionate Hearts

Edwards was one of the last of the *Puritans*; those English Christians of the sixteenth and seventeenth centuries who came to these shores and founded the first colonial settlements. While most Christians today have heard of the Puritans, there remains tremendous ignorance as to who they were and why it is important that we learn about them today. For many, the term *Puritan* drums up ideas of a pious individual who denies himself pleasure of any sort. In fact, the name is often associated with prudishness and sexual repression.

Yet these caricatures of the Puritans are a gross distortion of the facts. The Puritans were not only some of the greatest thinkers the English world has produced, they were extravagant lovers as well. Reading a Puritan writing regarding passionate love in marriage would make most Christians today blush.

The truth is, the more we study these Christians of a bygone era the more we will realize how much they have to teach us. They were eminent theologians who excelled in knowledge of God, producing some of the finest theological writings in Christian history. The Puritans thought deeply over the entire breadth of divine revelation. Reading a book like John Owen's *The Death of Death in the Death of Christ* or Richard Baxter's *The Reformed Pastor*, one is immediately convinced of the depth of their theological understanding. Yet the Puritans never studied theology merely to accumulate knowledge, but because of their belief that proper knowledge of God obtained through the study of Scripture and theology has a powerful effect on the heart.

Because the Puritans were great theologians, they also produced some of the finest preachers the English speaking world has ever known. According to the Puritans, an effective sermon must contain the twin elements of *light* and *heat*. By *light* they meant that every sermon must shed light on a biblical passage so that the hearers received knowledge of God or of themselves they did not previously possess. By *heat*, they meant that a sermon was not a theological lecture but a passionate declaration of the mind of God. Defining preaching in this way, it is not surprising that the Puritans produced such great preachers. Puritan sermons were rich in biblical and theological content, uttered from the lips of men consumed with desire to glorify God through the declaration of divine truth.

How different is this Puritan view of preaching, from what passes for preaching today—which focuses on stirring the emotions rather than helping people to understand God's Word. It is true that Puritan preaching stirred people's emotions as well. But it did not do so by manipulating people as many modern preachers do, but by faithfully expounding God's Word. It was as God's Word was taught through passionate and careful exposition that the Puritans stirred the emotions of their hearers.

Several years ago, I attended a popular revival conference where well-known revival preachers were scheduled to speak. As I listened to the various speakers in those meetings I was amazed at the total lack of biblical content in the messages. The preachers relied heavily on telling personal stories of miracles they had witnessed or talking about the revival which was occurring. There was virtually no exposition of Holy Scripture. Such preaching would have seemed strange to a man like Jonathan Edwards, who believed that true preaching only occurred when biblical theology was ignited by the Spirit of God.

Another important contribution of the English Puritans was *experiential* religion—the whole area of how the Holy Spirit applies the accomplishments of Christ's redemption to the hearts and lives of believers. Their literature reveals that they were masters of the religion of the heart. One of the greatest Puritan theologians to write on the Holy Spirit's work in the human heart was John Owen. His classic work *Pneumatology* is an exhaustive study of the Holy Spirit and his work in redemption. Owen wrote it not only because of his passionate belief that the Person and work of the Holy Spirit were central to the Reformation, but because of the two extremes he saw in the Church of his day— unbiblical *rationalism* on the one hand, which left little or no place for the Holy Spirit and *emotionalism* on the other, which placed too heavy an emphasis on the emotions. Since both are present in our own day, Owens' work along with that of many other Puritans has much to say to modern believers.

Thinking Feels Good

What can we hope to take away by studying the Puritans? Among other things, we learn from them that *thinking* is a spiritual act. The Puritans believed that the way to increased passion for God was *through* the mind. This seems strange to many moderns who are accustomed to viewing *thinking* as the opposite of *feeling*. It is also why intellectuals are regularly typecast as people who rarely show any emotion; as those who would much rather solve a mathematical problem or read an exacting volume than do something pleasurable.

Now there is no doubt that this accurately describes *some* intellectuals. Nevertheless, this should not lead us to conclude that intellectual exercise itself is synonymous with being emotionless. In reality, thinking deeply is an emotional exercise as author Everett Knight explains;

> "... thinking is rarely a matter of cold, heartless, calculating logic. *Thinking feels*. Sometimes when I am reading—and thinking while reading—my mind becomes so hot, so affected by the implications of the ideas, that I stop to cool off. John Henry Newman talks about the mind enraptured by the 'music of the spheres'. A. G. Sertillanges speaks of being lifted on the downy wings of truth. There is indeed a unity between thinking and feeling. Unity, in fact, stands behind all aspects of our human being" (*The Objective Society,* Everett Knight, pp.)

As Knight says, "there is indeed a unity between thinking and feeling." We in the West are so accustomed to separating the intellectual from the emotional that we tend to view them in opposition. Yet nowhere in Scripture do we find the idea that the intellectual and emotional aspects of human nature are opposed. Knight said it best; "Unity, in fact, stands behind all aspects of our human being." When it comes to real living the intellectual and emotional parts of us are integrally unified.

On more than one occasion I have listened to a preacher in a church service whose sole aim was to stir the emotions of the congregation. The preacher worked up the church members into a feverish pitch until emotions ran high. The excitement was not so much about the *content* of what was being spoken as much by the theatrics of the preacher. He manipulated their emotions and worked them up in the same way people are worked up at a pep rally or sporting event.

Correspondingly, there have been other times when I had the privilege of sitting under preaching which presented biblical truth with great clarity and power. Although the preacher did not aim at stirring his audience emotionally, the power of the ideas he presented actually had that effect. Whether speaking of the power of the blood of Jesus, the excellencies of Christ, or the glories of the New Covenant, our affections registered their pleasure as we contemplated these glorious themes through the preached word. It was at those times that I came away more fully understanding what the Psalmist meant when he said, "As I meditated, the fire burned" (Psalm 39:3).

Oswald Chambers was one who knew personally how that thinking deeply is vitally connected to passion for God. His biographer tells how a certain minister, sensing that his ministry was not what it should be, came to him asking him for advice. The man was surprised when Chambers asked him what books he was reading. Upon learning that he was reading only religious books, Chambers recommended some titles on topics such as philosophy, psychology, and history. It was not long afterwards that the man returned and told him that his entire life was changed by reading the books Chambers recommended. In his own words, he felt he had been "born again *again!*" Chambers was not surprised. He knew that what this man needed was to be stirred intellectually if he was to recover spiritual passion. That was why Chambers recommended those books in the first place.

It is vital that Christian leaders today learn to keep their own minds alive if they want to promote spiritual passion in the church. For those called to preach and teach the Word, this is non-negotiable. Far too much contemporary preaching lacks the kind of intellectual substance which not only feeds the mind, but stirs the emotions as well. God's people need solid substance if they are to learn to think deeply. We cannot expect those in the church to know the importance of developing their minds, if those handling the Word have not learned it themselves.

Worship: Enjoying God with Heart and Mind

One area of Christian service requiring the fullest use of our minds is *worship*. In no area are thinking and feeling more perfectly wedded than when we are engaged in the act of adoring our God. In worship, we bring both the fullness of our sanctified minds, and the richness of our affections to Him Who has redeemed us. Worship requires nothing less than the best of both if it is to be acceptable in His sight.

Much contemporary writing on worship today focuses on the cultivation of emotions, while ignoring entirely the importance of our worship being *intelligent*. By *intelligent*, I am not referring to worship which is offered by really smart people. Thankfully, our ability to worship properly is not dependent on our I.Q. Rather, I am speaking of the kind of worship Jesus described to the woman at the well—worship in "spirit and in *truth*" (John 4:24, italics mine). By worship in *spirit*, Jesus referred to the fact that worship only occurs when the human spirit actually encounters God. What did He mean by worship in truth? It was certainly more than that our worship must be sincere, but that it also must be properly *informed*. *True* worship is a response to God based on a proper apprehension of His essential nature and attributes. That is why worship and theology should never be separated. Only a high view of God will safeguard worship from being empty, ritualistic, or mere emotionalism.

Often, when attending some local church, I get the impression that the worship experience is more often about trying to achieve a certain feeling rather than glorifying God. The complete lack of theological content in many of the new worship songs today is a manifestation of this. Songs about "getting in the river" and "feeling God in this place" have replaced many of the hymns of the church which have lyrics extolling God's glory and sovereign ways. Lyrics such as, "All hail the power of Jesus name, let angels prostrate fall," when compared to the words of many of the modern worship ditties today, demonstrates how far down we've come. Other churches, on the other hand, are deathly afraid of expressing themselves emotionally in worship, believing that God is only glorified when emotion is totally left out of the worship experience. This also is not biblical. Are we to believe that the God who created us with the wonderful ability to *feel*, expects us to use this gift in every realm of life, but not when it comes to worship? Such an idea is ludicrous. God intends that we use our emotions in worship to the fullest, as we should do in every other arena of life. Yet, we must always do so with the awareness that the emotional side of worship can never to be separated from the intellectual.

So both (intellectual and emotional) are vital components of our worship of God. Yet ever and always, it is our knowledge of God gained from Scripture that should inform our worship. While it is true that the worshipper does experience God as he draws near, it is the greatness and majesty of God as perceived by the mind which is central to true worship. That is why the apostle Paul described worship as a *rational* exercise rather than an *emotional* experience (Romans 12:1). Yet, this fact (that the mind is central to true worship) must never be misconstrued so as to downplay the place of our emotions in worship. When we are singing songs extolling the greatness of God, it is hard not to be overcome with joy, thankfulness, and sheer amazement. Who can sit passively as he adores the extraordinary being of God?

The proper use of emotion in worship therefore, is a wonderful gift given to us by our heavenly Father. Scripture is replete with examples of how God's people experienced the full range of emotions during worship. My favorite is the story of how the older men wept uncontrollably when the foundation of the second temple was laid during the time of Ezra (Ezra 3:12). While these men wept, others shouted for joy in worship to God (Ezra 3:12). Certainly no one could blame them for such a display of emotion as they beheld the goodness of God to them in restoring them to the land and allowing them to rebuild His house.

Pleasures of the Mind

Where is *pleasure* located? In the mind or in the emotions? Usually, we think of pleasure as an emotion rather than something related to the exercise of the mind. Yet Scripture links pleasure directly to the working of the intellect. This doesn't mean that emotions aren't involved whenever we are experiencing pleasure, its just that pleasure is as much an intellectual exercise as it is an emotion.

This has incredible implications for us as believers. As we we learn to meditate on God in Scripture, we discover a source of pleasure only the sanctified mind can really understand. I learned this firsthand one day as I was reading the first Psalm. Psalm 1 serves as sort of a preface to the entire Psalter. As such, it sets forth the prominent theme running through the entire Psalter—the contrast between way of the righteous and the way of the wicked. The first Psalm begins by describing the things covenant men and women *don't* do because of their godliness (Psalm 1:1). In walking with God this is always the first lesson we must learn. When the life of God enters us through the new birth we instinctively know we can no longer walk as we once did, since we are called to a life of separation from the world. As a new believer, this was the first aspect of the sanctified life which I learned. I knew that now that I was saved, I could no longer live the way I formerly did. That's because everything about me was new.

But one day, while reading verse two of the Psalm, I realized that it not only teaches the things that righteous men and women don't do, but also describes what they *do*—they *delight* in meditating on the Law of God (Psalm 1:2). Studying the Hebrew word translated by the English word *delight* in this passage, I learned that it is often translated by the word *pleasure* in other Old Testament passages. At first I found that to be quite shocking. For me, pleasure characterized my old life, not my present life in Christ. Yet it was clear from verse two of the Psalm that the covenant man or woman is known by the great pleasure he or she derives from meditating upon God's Word.

This discovery deeply challenged my previous commitment to Scripture. Until that time I was very disciplined to read my Bible every day, but I did so largely out of a sense of duty rather than from the pleasure I derived from it. But the first Psalm (along with other passages of Scripture such as Psalm 119 which contains one hundred and seventy six verses extolling the virtue of God's written revelation) now challenged me to a new relationship to Holy Scripture. Bible reading could never again be about simply fulfilling a legal obligation; rather, I must learn to deeply meditate upon Scripture so that the full weight of God's glory might be known.

I soon learned that if I wanted to make progress in sanctification, I must allow my mind to be so occupied with Him that my soul actually feasts on Him. It is only the degree to which I treasure God's Word that I will actually desire not to sin, as author Sam Storms points out:

> "All of us want to not sin. That's why I wrote this book and that is why you're reading it. The apostle Paul said in Romans 3:23 that 'all have sinned and fall short of the glory of God,' by which I take him to mean that sin is failing to glorify God because of having cherished other things as more valuable and enjoyable than He. The key to not sinning is therefore to enjoy God above all else, for in our enjoyment of Him is His glory in us. The psalmist declares that the way not to sin, that is, the way to enjoy God above all else, is by treasuring His Word in our hearts (Psalm 119:11). Making God's Word our heart's treasure is another way of describing one aspect of meditation. More than merely 'confessing' His Word, 'treasuring' it 'in our hearts means placing ultimate value on its truth, prizing it as something precious and dear of

supreme excellence, and then ingesting it through memorization and meditation so that it flows freely through our spiritual veins. When this happens, the Holy Spirit energizes our hearts to believe and behave in conformity with its dictates. In other words, we sin less" (*Pleasures Evermore*, Sam Storms, page 186).

This emphasis (that pleasure is achieved by meditation on God's Word) must be recaptured in the Church today. It is only as we learn to use our minds in this way that we will make progress in the sanctified life. That's because God ordained the mind to be the great *pleasure* center. David understood this when he declared, "As I meditated the fire burned" (Psalm 39:3). Proper meditation on God and His Word therefore not only leads to a greater understanding of God's Word, but a "warming" of our affections as well.

The English Puritans understood this, which is why they made no apology for their lavish display of affection in their religious life (as well as in their marital relationships). They were some of the most passionate people ever to grace this planet precisely because they trained their minds to deeply meditate on Scripture. Reading a Puritan work of theology one is struck not only by the depth of their understanding of Scripture, but by their rich devotional style as well.

What Lies Ahead

We will never see a restoration of passion for truth in the Church unless we first recapture this biblical emphasis on the place of the mind in Christian living. Sadly, mindlessness is not only endemic of our age in general, but also of much of the modern Western Church as well. The only remedy is the emergence of a generation of Christians who know how to think properly to the glory of God. Yet to do so, they will first have to rid themselves of unscriptural ideas regarding the mind, which have formed many of our understandings of Christian spirituality. May God give to his Church in this hour a new passion to think deeply for the glory of His name and the advancement of His kingdom. Amen.

As we move into the third and final section of this book, we will examine some practical ways in which passion for truth can be cultivated in the Church today. The three chapters in that section deal with such things as the important place doctrine holds in creating spiritual passion, the importance of preaching as a means of promoting passion for truth, and the relationship of biblical truth to the Person of Christ. In a sense, much of the material in the final section deals with the *church's* role in promoting passion for truth. Paul speaks of the church as the "pillar and support of the truth" (I Timothy 3:15). As such, God has ordained certain *means* by which passion for truth is to be both inaugurated and maintained in the house of God. Using these means properly goes a long way in restoring a passion for truth to the people of God.

A PASSION FOR TRUTH

CHAPTER EIGHT

That Dirty Word, 'Doctrine'

Mention the word *doctrine* in some quarters of the Body of Christ today and you might think you'd uttered an expletive. Doctrine has fallen on hard times in many churches. For some believers, doctrine is viewed as that which restricts the life and freedom of the Spirit in the church. The "spiritual" believer today is portrayed as the one who pursues experiences with God rather, than the one seeking to understand biblical doctrine.

It is not surprising therefore, that many believers today are doctrinally *illiterate*. Few churches find their members beating the doors down to learn doctrine. They will come out to hear titillating testimonies or the latest prophetic mystery; yet when it comes to learning sound biblical instruction, they are not to be found. Instead of giving their members an appetite for biblical doctrine, many churches seem more concerned with entertaining their members than feeding them with solid, biblical instruction.

Why is there such an aversion to learning doctrine in the Church today? For one, many believe that Christian growth occurs primarily through the accumulation of spiritual experiences rather than by learning God's Word. Why bother to learn the propositions of Scripture, when we can learn by direct experience with God?

To be fair, God does teach us much through the experiences He is pleased to give us. The Christian life itself begins with a new birth in which the Spirit brings a person into *personal* knowledge of God, and that is infinitely more than mere intellectual apprehension of biblical truth. So the view that we can learn much from our experiences is certainly biblical. Nevertheless, true Christianity cannot be divorced from those biblical propositions which define it. They (biblical propositions) are to Christianity what a foundation is to a building—separate the faith from these propositions, and you reduce it to little more than one of the many private spiritualities so popular in America today. To be opposed to doctrine therefore, is to negate the very essence of the Christian faith.

People who disparage doctrine often forget that the word 'doctrine' simply means 'teaching.' When Scripture speaks of doctrine it is referring to that body of truth committed to the apostles by the Lord Jesus Christ from which the Christian faith is defined. To say that doctrine doesn't matter therefore, is to say that what Jesus Christ and the apostles taught is unimportant. Are we really prepared to say that?

Defining doctrine as that body of teaching given to the apostles by the Lord, helps us to understand something. While there is a wealth of teaching in the church today dealing with every conceivable topic under the sun, there is a dearth of doctrinal substance in much of that teaching. For example, one can hear many messages in the Church today containing veiled references to the blood of Jesus—how the blood cleanses from sin or how Satan hates the blood of Christ, etc. Yet one can hear all of this teaching without ever learning anything about the doctrine of the atonement. That's because to understand the doctrine of the atonement, one must understand such things as God's justice and his holy wrath against sin—subjects rarely taught in the Church today. So while people in our churches might hear mention of the blood of Jesus, few learn what the doctrine of the atonement means and how it applies to our lives.

Another reason for the doctrinal malaise found in the Church today is the widely accepted but mistaken belief that doctrine is primarily *intellectual* in nature. Since the mind is viewed as the least important faculty in the development of Christian spirituality, few see any need to learn doctrinal truth. What they fail to perceive, though, is that there is a close correspondence between what a person believes (doctrine) and how he or she lives. In other words, doctrine is not just for the mind; it affects how we live. Reading the pastoral letters (I and II Timothy, Titus, Philemon) it becomes clear that there is a close connection between doctrine and life. Nowhere in these letters does Paul suggest that doctrine is mere academic information unrelated to life, but 'life-giving' truth which applies to every area of human life. For the apostle, there was no contradiction between theology and practical Christian living. One led naturally to the other.

Another reason for the lack of interest to learn doctrine in the Church today is the mistaken belief that by having no doctrinal beliefs we exhibit a greater openness to what the Spirit wants to teach us. This is wrong for at least two reasons. First, Scripture nowhere equates doctrinal unsettledness with openness to the Spirit. While it is true that we may not know all that Scripture teaches at any given time, we can (and must) be *settled* when it comes to our understanding of basic doctrinal truth. The idea that by having no settled beliefs, we thereby demonstrate a greater openness to the Spirit finds no justification at all in Scripture.

The other reason this view is wrong, is that the notion of a 'doctrine-less' faith is pure myth. Everyone *has* doctrine—the only question is whether they have *sound* doctrine or *unsound* doctrine (teachings not based on Scripture). Those who boast of being 'doctrine-free' often believe and teach things contrary to Scripture even while claiming to be without doctrine. So this claim to be doctrine-free is bogus.

When defining doctrine as the life-giving truth given by Jesus Christ to the apostles it becomes obvious that learning doctrine is an important component of Christian living. Every church desirous of producing healthy believers must establish them on the the sound doctrines of the faith. Jesus made it clear that making disciples entails building lives on the truth of what He taught (Matthew 28:19-20). Only by establishing men and women on this foundation, can they ever hope to live fruitful lives which glorify God. Learning the truth of Scripture therefore is infinitely more than a mere academic exercise.

False Ideas Regarding Doctrine in the Church Today

The place to begin in combatting the doctrinal malaise in the Church today, is to first negate some of the false ideas regarding doctrine that are currently in vogue. I briefly mentioned a few at the beginning of this chapter. I want to now focus on four others which are wildly popular throughout the body of Christ today. They are: the belief that doctrine is the cause of much of the division in the Church, that sincerity rather than accuracy is what really matters when it comes to our beliefs, that our faith should be in the Person of Christ rather than specific doctrines about Him and finally, the rise of Christian *pragmatism*—that faith is driven by what works rather than what is true. A brief description of each follows.

Doctrine divides

A belief that many Christians hold today, and which has gained almost cult-like status is the notion that doctrine is the source of most of the divisions existing in the church. Since (according to this view) doctrine promotes divisions, believers should focus on "loving one another" rather than attempting to agree on doctrinal matters. Attempting to agree when it comes to doctrine will only foster divisions and breed contention. So, we should make loving Jesus and one another the most important thing.

Now on the surface this view has much to commend it. The New Testament lays great stress on the need for believers to love one another and maintain the unity of the Spirit (Ephesians 4:3). We are to renounce rancor, ill-will, and the pride which so easily divides us. The cause of Christ has been greatly damaged by the refusal of believers to walk in that love and unity which alone convinces the world we are his disciples (John 13:35). We cannot escape our culpability in this matter.

At the same time, it does appear as if doctrine is responsible for much of the division existing in the Church today. We have all heard horror stories of how doctrinal differences have split a church or broken up a citywide prayer meeting. Five hundred years ago Luther and Zwingli, two men who largely agreed on most things pulled away from each other after disagreeing about the precise nature of Christ's presence in the Lord's Supper—a matter which arguably is not even addressed in Scripture. Some groups today will not fellowship with other groups because of the manner in which they baptize, or their particular eschatological view. So at least on the surface, it does appear as if doctrine has contributed much to the disunity in the Church today.

Yet that is only how it appears on the surface. In reality, doctrine is not responsible for our division. Blaming doctrine for our disunity is really a convenient scapegoat which allows us to avoid placing the blame where it really belongs—on our lack of *maturity*. Blaming doctrine for our disunity is like blaming the vision chart at an optometrist office for our poor eyesight. If we can't read the chart it's not because something's wrong with the chart but with our eyesight. The chart simply allows us to discover the problem. Even so, doctrinal differences in the Church do not tell us that there is a problem with doctrine, but illuminate the fact that that we don't *see* clearly when it comes to divine truth. Instead of disparaging doctrine, we should be asking God for greater light when it comes to understanding Holy Scripture.

Far from teaching that doctrine divides, Scripture *actually* teaches that it is only by embracing doctrinal truth that true unity can be achieved. In the Ephesian letter, Paul speaks of the "unity of the faith" (Ephesians 4:13). By "faith" in this passage, Paul is not referring to *personal* belief in Jesus but to the core doctrines which define the Christian faith. Jude speaks of the "faith once delivered to the saints" in the letter he wrote (Jude 3). We learn from these passages that it is only by firmly holding to this body of truth that true and lasting unity can be realized. In biblical terms, truth *unifies* rather than divides.

That is why it is vital that our churches be places where doctrine is not only properly taught, but also where doctrinal differences are discussed in an atmosphere of love and forbearance. Many believers are surprised to learn that before the advent of television and radio, men would meet together to vigorously debate theological issues. They viewed these debates not only as a means of educating themselves in the truth of the Gospel, but of entertainment as well. There were often sharp disagreements, yet they would never allow these to be a cause for division. The Puritans are a good example of this. No group of Christians ever had more lively theological discussions yet they were always conducted with the utmost Christian charity.

Sadly, we avoid such theological discussions today for fear that people will be offended and divisions will be fostered. Yet in so doing we rob ourselves of a major means of being educated in the faith. I have personally profited greatly from times of doctrinal discussion, even with those I vehemently disagreed with. Such discussions have gone a long way in helping me to understand the body of Christ (not to mention helping me to clarify my own positions). We need not fear that such doctrinal discussions will automatically foster division. The real issue is whether we possess the maturity to handle our disagreements.

Sincere doctrine is the same as sound doctrine

Another common belief today is that *sincere* doctrine is the same as sound doctrine. According to this view, *sincerity* rather than *accuracy* is what is most important when it comes to what we believe. In other words, God accepts people based on how *sincere* they are in their beliefs rather than how accurate their views are.

Now Scripture certainly places great value on sincerity. Paul tells Timothy that the goal of Gospel instruction is the development of a *sincere* faith (I Timothy 1:5). Paul himself has sweet remembrances of the *sincere* faith which dwelt in Timothy as a result of his grandmother and mother's influence (II Timothy 1:5). The writer of Hebrews exhorts his readers to "draw near to God with a *sincere* heart" (Hebrews 10:22). And the apostle Peter, when speaking of the new birth, reminds his readers that it has produced a "*sincere* love for the brethren" in their hearts (I Peter 1:22). All of these passages make clear that sincerity is an important component of Christian living.

Yet notice that in all these passages there is no reference to *sincere* doctrine. That's because when it comes to doctrine it is not sincerity but *accuracy* which matters most. We may be totally sincere in what we believe but if it is not accurate, all of our sincerity counts for nothing—we are sincerely wrong! More times than I wish to acknowledge, I have found myself driving on a certain road, convinced it would take me to my destination, only to later discover I was *sincerely* wrong (and having to admit it to my wife). All my sincerity mattered nothing; if I had stayed on that road I would not have arrived at my destination. In the same way, we may be sincerely persuaded that what we believe is taught in Scripture, even though it is not at all what God's Word teaches.

This idea that sincerity rather than accuracy matters most when it comes to our handling of Scripture has seriously undermined the study of the Scriptures in the Church today. Why bother digging deeply into God's word if, after all, He is not really concerned with accuracy? We might as well hold to our beliefs without bothering to check if they are biblical. That is, in fact, what many today are doing.

The truth is, even those who claim to believe that sincerity rather than accuracy matters most, don't live by their belief. When a member of the Watchtower Society or a Mormon shows up at their door, suddenly accuracy matters, and they will do everything in their power to turn them from false doctrine to orthodox Christian beliefs. If doctrine really *does* matter when it comes to distinguishing true believers from false, why doesn't it matter when it comes to other areas of church life as well? The truth is, it does.

Our faith should be in Christ, not doctrine

The phrase, "No Creed, But Christ" sums up the third reason for the decline of desire to learn doctrine in the Church today. This is the view that says our faith should not be in specific doctrines, but in Christ Himself. In other words, our faith should not so much be in the Bible, but in a *Person*.

Now it is true that Scripture teaches that we are not merely to believe certain things *about* Jesus, but believe *in* Jesus Himself. A person enters a relationship with God by gaining knowledge of God and Christ through the working of the Holy Spirit. That means that there is a wide gulf between knowing the Bible and possessing personal knowledge of God. A person might have a thorough knowledge of Scripture without possessing any real knowledge of God Himself. So we must never equate mere Bible knowledge with personal knowledge of God. Nevertheless, while it is true that knowledge of God entails more than mere possession of biblical propositions, neither can it be defined *apart* from those propositions. True faith is based solidly upon what God has stated in Scripture regarding His Son. The idea that our faith should be in Christ rather than in what Scripture asserts about Him ignores the fact that intellectual conviction is an important part of genuine faith.

The goal of knowing Scripture therefore, is to lead us to a thorough conviction about Christ so that we may commit ourselves to Him. Why did God go to the bother of providing us with a written revelation in the first place, if not for the fact that it (Scripture) provides us with an *objective* body of truth about Christ so that we might be able to put our trust in Him? While the goal of faith must be a living relationship with Jesus, it must always be a relationship with the Christ revealed in Scripture. Any departure from that standard is a deviation from the faith, and is to be rejected.

The truth is, we are called to both believe *in* Jesus as well as believe the biblical propositions *about* Him. Since these two are never at odds, we should not fear that faith in biblical truth will hinder us from knowing

Christ Himself. I once talked to a believer who felt that knowledge of Scripture might actually hinder a person from a *true* knowledge of God. He cited, as evidence of this, the passage in Matthew 2:1-8 where King Herod inquired of the Jewish scribes as to where Messiah was to be born (he cited Scripture in order to prove that Scripture isn't necessary). His point was that while the scribes gave Herod a perfectly biblical answer, they themselves did not actually go there to seek him. In his mind, this proved that Bible knowledge might actually hinder one from knowing Christ Himself.

Yet this man was mistaken in his application of this story. The problem with the scribes was not that Scriptural knowledge kept them from Christ; it was that they had no real faith in Him to begin with. If they had really believed that Jesus was the Messiah, they would most certainly have joined the wise men in searching for him at Bethlehem. While this story does demonstrate that it is possible to possess knowledge of Scripture without having a *real* knowledge of the Son, it in no way teaches that knowledge of Scripture actually hinders one from knowing Him.

The new religion of pragmatism

Another reason for doctrinal malaise in the Church today is the steady rise in the West of *Pragmatism*. Pragmatism is attributed to William James, a twentieth century philosopher who formulated its basic tenets. James taught that things have no intrinsic value apart from the utilitarian purpose which they serve. By its very definition therefore, Pragmatism is anti-philosophical (though it is itself a philosophy). Pragmatists have no interest in understanding *why* things are the way they are; they leave all such meanderings to philosophers and theologians. Pragmatists are only interested in what *works*. It is therefore the ultimate utilitarian mindset.

Pragmatism is now the functional religion of America in the twenty-first century. Most Americans are interested in what works— what they can use that will make their lives better. They give little thought to *why* things are the way they are. Pragmatism has given us so many of the technological advances we have come to rely on. Can you imagine what life would be like today without computers or microwaves or digital cameras or the ability to board a plane on the East coast and be on the West coast in a few hours? America has become the most innovative culture the world has ever known, due largely to the rise of Pragmatism.

Now there is nothing intrinsically wrong with the desire to be more productive. Our forebears were not better off because they read by candlelight or died without many of the scientific breakthroughs which make it possible for humans to live longer today. The problem is not with being *pragmatic*, but *Pragmatism*—the belief that things have no intrinsic value *unless* they provide some benefit to us. It is this idea, that things have no value apart from what they do, that puts it in direct conflict with Scripture.

Sadly, the Church itself has not escaped the influence of Pragmatism. A form of *Christian* Pragmatism is in vogue today which views faith largely in terms of how it benefits the one who believes rather than whether it is true. Influenced by Pragmatism, many evangelists today sound more like slick salesmen playing up the benefits of their product in order to make a sale, than men of God preaching the everlasting Gospel. Even the teaching ministry of the Church has not been able to avoid the influence of Pragmatism. The last thirty years has seen the emergence of a cottage industry of so-called 'practical teaching' dealing with every conceivable subject under the sun, much of which teaches people how to make their lives better. The end result is that people pick and choose the teachings they like based on their perception of what will benefit them most. Entire portions of Scripture are thus ignored since they are viewed as irrelevant to the ultimate purpose of bettering their lives.

Pragmatism has definitely had an effect on how leaders handle the Word of God today. Pastors and teachers are called to teach the entire breadth of Scripture not just those portions of Scripture they personally like. Yet if they are guided by pragmatism they will naturally avoid those portions of Scripture which they consider to be irrelevant or offensive. Faithful leaders though will not shrink from teaching these things, even at the risk of offending some. They will settle in their hearts that they are called to teach the entire truth regardless of whether or not those in the congregation consider it important.

The Need for Sound Doctrine

In his letters, the apostle Paul exhorts church leaders to uphold and teach *sound* doctrine. Paul understood that teaching the sound doctrines of the faith was a critical component of ensuring that local churches remained healthy. For that reason, he insisted that leaders give careful attention to teaching that body of truth given to the apostles, and which is now recorded for us in Holy Scripture. According to Paul, the only way individuals and churches can maintain spiritual health is by feeding upon the sound doctrines of the faith.

Several years ago, I became concerned about my physical health, and determined to live a healthier lifestyle. The first thing I did was educate myself about those foods which promoted healthy living. I learned the importance of taking in foods rich in nutrients rather than foods with no nutritional value. Of course it took more than simply learning about those foods to make a difference. I had to actually change my diet before I could expect any measurable results. As I began to apply what I had learned, I began to feel stronger and healthier. In the same way, if we want to live healthy Christian lives we must be concerned with our spiritual diet—those things we are feeding upon and building our churches and lives upon. We must make sure that our diet is based on a rich feeding of God's Word.

One of the clearest passages setting forth the relationship between sound doctrine and healthy Christian is found in the New Testament letter to the Ephesians, chapter four verses eleven through sixteen. It begins with Paul enumerating the five gifted ministries whose task it is to 'equip the saints for the work of ministry' (4:11). According to the apostle, it is only as God's people are properly equipped through these ministries that they achieve spiritual maturity—a maturity evidenced chiefly by doctrinal *stability* (4:14). He characterizes the mature as those not "tossed about by every *wave* of doctrine." Boat owners are well acquainted with the image the apostle uses in this passage. If a boat brought to dock is not immediately anchored it will easily drift from shore by the gentle force of the waves. According to Paul, false teaching carries away those who are not well anchored to the shoreline of doctrinal certainty. The writer to the Hebrews also uses this metaphor when exhorting his readers to "pay close attention to what you have heard so that you don't *drift* away from it" (Hebrews 2:1). The only safeguard against this tendency is to give careful attention to what they had *already* heard—the Gospel which had already been preached to them.

Both of these passages teach the importance of having *settled* views of Christian truth. As mentioned previously, some Christians believe that by having no settled views of truth they are exhibiting a greater openness to what the Spirit wants to teach them at any time. That was certainly the view I had after first coming to faith. I thought that if I had no firm beliefs to speak of, I was remaining open to the teaching of the Spirit. It was later that I realized the danger of this view. By embracing it, I was (unknowingly) accepting the idea that the Spirit and the Word were at variance. I soon learned that Scripture teaches that these are never at odds. That meant that the Spirit would always leads me *to* doctrinal certainty, not *from* it.

The great nineteenth century English preacher Charles Spurgeon understood this well. In his classic work on preaching (Lectures to My Students) Spurgeon tells of his interview with a young man who had applied as a candidate to his Pastor's College. Thinking to impress Spurgeon during the interview, the young man told him he had no fixed doctrinal beliefs. Upon hearing this, Spurgeon immediately denied him entrance into the college. In his view, a man who had not settled the most basic doctrines of Scripture was unfit to be a minister of the Gospel:

> "When young fellows say that they have not made up their minds upon theology, they ought to go back to the Sunday-school until they have. For a man to come shuffling into a College, pretending that he holds his mind open to any form of truth, and that he is eminently receptive, but has not settled in his mind such things as whether God has an election of grace, or whether he loves his people to the end, seems to me a perfect monstrosity" (*Lectures to My Students*, Charles Spurgeon, pg.)

What would Spurgeon say about the vast numbers of leaders today who are totally illiterate when it comes to the most basic Bible doctrines? I am sure he would not be impressed. He would view our attitude towards doctrine in the modern Church as nothing less than doctrinal compromise.

Laying a Doctrinal Foundation

Since sound doctrine is so critical to healthy Christian living, establishing disciples in biblical truth is one of the most important things a local church can do. Throughout the ages, churches have chosen to do this in various ways. By far, the most popular has been the *catechism*; a series of questions and answers used to test people's religious knowledge in advance of Christian baptism or confirmation. Some of the most popular catechisms became crystallized into the various Confessions which have come down to our day. One of the most popular is the Westminster Confession, famous for its question, "What is chief end of man?" to which the Confession answers, "The chief end of man is to glorify God and enjoy Him forever." While Westminster is known as a *Confession*, it was originally written as a classic catechism.

Most churches today reject the use of catechisms to establish disciples in biblical truth, viewing them as archaic remnants of an bygone era. Yet they have not replaced catechisms with any meaningful alternative of grounding their members in sound doctrine. My own experience is evidence of this. After entering my first church after my conversion, I was handed a Bible and told to read the Gospel of John. So I was left entirely on my own to figure out the teachings of the Bible. In the long run this turned out to be a blessing in disguise in that it forced me to learn to seek out doctrinal substance for myself. Still, I would have fared much better if I had learned sound doctrine from my church rather than being left entirely on my own to figure out what the Bible taught.

If we are to take seriously the Great Commission mandate to "make disciples of all nations" (Matthew 28:18-20) we must do more than merely hand people Bibles and tell them to read them. At the core of the Commission is the command to teach disciples *all* that Jesus commanded (28:19). Therefore, we must have a *systematic* approach to teaching people; one that guarantees that disciples are learning all that Jesus taught. A haphazard approach simply will not accomplish this. By a *systematic* approach I do not mean one which starts with certain beliefs and then forces Scripture to conform, but a study which compares 'Scripture to Scripture' so that the basic doctrines of God's Word are easily grasped. Far from obscuring the meaning of Scripture, this approach allows us to discover the true meaning of Scripture.

In actuality, even those who protest the most against this type of approach practice it themselves. For example, when they make a statement like 'God loves His people', they are not actually quoting Scripture, but summarizing the teaching of Scripture drawn from many passages. If only one text taught it they might not be able to speak of it authoritatively, but since several texts speak of it, they are able to teach it fully assured that it is what Scripture says. This is what is meant by a systematic study of Scripture.

Sadly, few churches today actually teach the Scriptures in this manner. People are taught to read the Bible devotionally, but they are not taught to study it so as to gain a proper understanding of its teachings. Whereas systematic study was once considered to be a major means of establishing new converts in the faith, it is no longer the case.

Consequently, many of God's people remain strangers to the most important doctrines of Scripture, which has contributed greatly to the loss of passion for truth in God's house.

Learning the Doctrines of Grace

Which are the most important biblical doctrines believers should learn? Without a doubt, those doctrines of God's Word from which we derive our understanding of God's grace are among the most importnat. They deal with God's work of eternal redemption through His Son Jesus Christ and its application to our lives. Understanding these doctrines is not only essential for personal spiritual growth, but for the continued advancement of the Gospel in the earth as well. Paul speaks of the increase of the Gospel which resulted from the Colossians' hearing and understanding "God's grace in all its truth" (Colossians 1:6). That means that the secret of the Colossians' growth, as well as their ability to advance the Gospel, was their own growth in understanding of the grace of God which comes through the Gospel. And our own spiritual growth, as well as the advancement of the kingdom in the earth today, requires that we also grow in our understanding of the grace of the Gospel.

Viewed in this light, it is tragic that many believers today remain woefully ignorant of the truth of God's grace. They have been taught the things they should practice certain for spiritual growth such as prayer, commitment, giving, service. But because they have not been taught the truth of the grace of God, these things begin to be viewed as stepping stones to God rather than acts performed as the result of a changed nature. And even the practice of these things themselves become burdensome having not been sweetened by the grace of the Gospel. The end result is that they live lives characterized by frustration and hopelessness rather than the righteousness, peace, and joy which are the fruits of the Gospel.

For that reason, it is incumbent on churches today to teach new converts the truth of God's grace from the moment they enter the kingdom. This is especially important for church leaders; they must teach the truth of God's grace both publicly and privately so that new believers can grow in an atmosphere of grace. Yet first they must confront the fear that teaching the truth of God's grace will encourage *licentiousness*; distorting God's grace so that it become a license to sin.

Since the first century, when false prophets and teachers distorted the true grace of God so as to justify their ungodly lifestyles, this has been a problem for the body of Christ (see Jude 4). Yet the fault does not lie in teaching of the grace of God. Far from encouraging sin, the truth of God's grace actually creates a passion for God's glory that compels us to please Him in all things. As the realization of all that God in Christ has done for us dawns on us, our hearts respond with a desire to give ourselves unreservedly to Him (Romans 12:1-2). The implications couldn't be clearer. If we want churches filled with holy people, we must make sure that the truth of God's grace is not only preached from our pulpits, but taught to all new disciples as well.

Chief among these doctrines that we must know and teach is the doctrine of 'justification by faith alone.' Martin Luther referred to this doctrine as "the article upon which the church of God stands or falls." I don't think Luther over-exaggerated the importance of this doctrine for the life of the Church. It certainly held that place in his own life. After years of attempting to find peace with God through religious works, the truth that God justifies sinners through faith *alone* released him from self-serving bondage into the glorious liberty of the children of God, and in the process spawned one of the mightiest spiritual revolutions the world has ever known—the Protestant Reformation. Thus, from one man who discovered the truth of God's grace, millions of captives were released from bondage and restored to a God-centered existence.

When people are not well established in the truth of God's justifying grace, their lives reflect it. I saw this firsthand while serving on the pastoral staff of a local church. Each week, I prayed at the altar with those who regularly responded to the pastor's messages. Many of these people were requesting prayer to rid themselves of the gnawing feeling that all was not right between them and God. Before praying, I often asked if they understood the doctrine of justification by faith. What I found is that many of these saints were completely unfamiliar with this doctrine even though they had been in the church for many years. Unable to talk to them at length at the altar, I encouraged them to see me in the coming week so we could have more time to discuss it. That following week my calendar was filled with appointments in which I instructed people in the truth of the grace of God.

There is a great need that this doctrine be taught throughout the worldwide body of Christ today. Much of what passes for the Gospel in many churches today is a hodgepodge of religious ideas and moralisms mixed in with the Gospel of God. No wonder God's people feel so un-settled! Being strangers to God's grace they end up on the performance treadmill, attempting to earn from God what can only be given as a gift. Only a true knowledge of what God did in Christ deals a deathblow to this 'performance trap.' That's because it alone (the truth of God's grace) deals with the real problem of our guilt before a holy God.

The realization that God in Christ has fully and completely par-doned us so that our sins can never again be called into judgment, frees our consciences from what the writer of Hebrews called "dead works" to serve the living God (Hebrews 9:14). Incidentally, the term 'dead works' in the above text refers to those ritual services required under the Law of Moses, which could never really take away sin. While few believers today are practicing the ritual services prescribed under the Law of Moses, many engage in their own version of "dead works" in an attempt to rid themselves of guilt. Only the truth of God's grace, though, will free them to look outside of themselves to the God Who justifies.

This truth, that God justifies sinners through the finished work of the Lord Jesus Christ, was foreshadowed in the Old Testament by an elabo-rate ritual God told Moses to perform on the eve of their departure from Egypt. In connection with the final plague (the death of the firstborn of Egypt) each Israelite family was commanded to take from the flock a one year old male lamb without blemish. They were then to separate it from the flock on the tenth day of the month of Nisan and keep it till the fourteenth (Exodus 12:1-5). On the fourteenth day, the head of a household was to slay their lamb applying some of its blood to the lintel and doorposts of their home (Exodus 12:6-7). As each Israelite family obeyed they received the assurance that the death angel would *passover* that house (12:13).

How did the Israelites know the blood of the lamb would protect them from God's wrath? They didn't, except for the fact that God had declared it to them. It was as they trusted what God had said, that they were assured judgment would pass over them. This is evident from the fact that once the blood was applied to the outside of each home, those inside were unable to see it. Yet it really didn't matter; after all, the blood was not for them, but for God ("when I *see* the blood, I will pass over you"). By faith, each Israelite family had to trust God's valuation of the blood.

The same thing is true of those who who have been redeemed by blood far more precious than that of Passover lambs (I Peter 1:18-19). We also must trust God's valuation of the blood of His Son, that it is precious in his sight and the means by which we are made acceptable to God. It is as we do so that we experience the power of that blood to cleanse us from *all* sin (I John 1:9).

Along with justification by faith alone is the doctrine of total depravity as well as the doctrine of election. Time will not allow a thorough description of each of these here. It is vital that believers learn all of the truth regarding God's grace today. These doctrines direct our attention to the objective truth of God, regarding the finished work of His Son. Being grounded in the objective truth of the Gospel is the only way we make spiritual progress in our Christian lives. May the truth of God's grace be proclaimed in every church so that God's people are released to live God-centered lives, bringing glory to His name. Amen.

CHAPTER NINE

Is There a Preacher
in the House?

On more than one occasion, I have had someone report to me a church service they attended where they witnessed God moving in an extraordinary way. Almost without exception, the thing they cited as evidence that "God was in control of the service" was that the people continuing worshipping so that the preacher was unable to give his sermon. This fact (that the preacher couldn't give his sermon) was considered as a clear token that the Lord had visited the church in a special way.

Now, I have no intrinsic problem with the notion that God might so move in a church service as to interrupt the normal order of service. In fact, I have been in church services where this has occurred, so I have no problem with it conceptually. Even Scripture itself seems to allow for it. The Old Testament records how that when Solomon dedicated the first temple, the priests were unable to enter to perform their duties because of the presence of the glory of God (I Kings 5:13-14). Instead of ministering in the sanctuary, they fell on their faces and worshipped throughout the entire service. Since God has done this in the past, I see no intrinsic reason that such a thing can't happen in the present.

Still, whenever I hear such reports I am uncomfortable. I can't help feeling that the reason for my uncomfortableness, is that behind these reports is the subtle (or not so subtle) belief that when God is really moving, preaching can be dispensed with. Perhaps this is a reflection on how little we really value preaching. Why is it that in over thirty years of hearing such reports I have never heard someone say they attended a church service where God moved so powerfully, that worship was dispensed with so that preaching might commence? I'm sure it has happened; it's just that in over thirty years of ministry I have never heard about it.

I am convinced that there is a general devaluing of preaching in the church today. We simply are no longer convinced that preaching is a major means of furthering His kingdom. It is evident in some of the things we say about preaching such as, "If preaching could save the world, it would have already been saved." The inference is that preaching has failed and we must look elsewhere if we want to see people converted. We say these things, even though they are at variance with the plain teaching of Scripture that preaching is God's ordained means of saving the world.

One reason for the general devaluing of preaching in the Church is the belief that *postmoderns* will no longer tolerate it. We are told that Postmoderns won't accept someone forcing his or her views on others. We are told that we must now find other ways of communicating the message if we want to be heard. This has led some churches to abandon the term 'sermon' for a 'time of sharing,' a much less imposing term. The pulpit itself is no longer viewed as a place where an authoritative message is proclaimed, but where various ideas are shared. This is a clear departure from Scripture which presents preaching not simply as the sharing of an idea, but a spoken word carrying with it the authority of God Himself. To make it anything else is to distort it into something less than what Scripture says it is.

But by far, the most insidious way preaching is devalued in the Church today is by failing to distinguish it from *pulpiteering*, a term I first became acquainted with when reading Dr. Martyn Lloyd Jones' classic work on preaching, 'Preachers and Preaching.' According to Dr. Lloyd Jones, *pulpiteering* is the act of using a pulpit in order to move people not so much by *what* is being said, but by *how* it is conveyed. Whereas biblical preaching is *content*-driven, pulpiteers seek to move people through their *manner* rather than their *matter*. This is how it differs from biblical preaching. Pulpiteers are more concerned with *how* they deliver the sermon than with what they are saying. This is important so I will deal with it more fully later in this chapter.

Preach the Word

When we compare the modern view of preaching with that of Holy Scripture, the difference is obvious. Holy Scripture places great priority on preaching as both the means of spreading the Gospel as well as feeding and sustaining the Church of God. Not only is this taught by direct injunction (II Timothy 4:2), it is apparent through various biblical examples. The Lord's forerunner John the Baptist came primarily as a 'preacher' of good news. During his earthly ministry, the Lord Jesus Himself came as a *preacher*, heralding the arrival of the kingdom of God to Israel. And when He trained his apostles he sent them into the world primarily as preachers of good news (Mark 3:14). Preaching was not peripheral to their work—it was their work! And the same is true for those God calls into the ministry today. He intends that preaching also be their lifework.

A number of years ago, I taught a series of messages in our local church from the book of Second Timothy. This is the last letter penned by the apostle Paul before being martyred by the Roman emperor Nero. It is one of the letters (along with First Timothy and Titus) commonly classified as *pastoral;* correspondence written to young pastors whom Paul personally mentored. What is often overlooked though, is that the twin letters to Timothy contain powerful prophetic utterances regarding the peril facing the church in the last days (II Timothy 3:1). Paul's purpose in these prophecies was to prepare Timothy for the real crisis about to come upon the churches of Asia at that time. Viewed in this light, it is interesting to read Paul's description of the *nature* of the peril which these churches were facing. He mentions none of the things usually associated with *peril* in relation to the last days—nuclear war, political and economic disasters, pestilence, disease, and the rise of the Antichrist. Instead, he focuses on the total dissolution of moral character as the real evidence that the last days had arrived (read II Timothy 3:1-9).

Why is Paul's description of the last days so different from that of many modern day prophecy teachers? The answer is simple: His purpose was not to titillate, but to prepare Timothy and the churches he served for the real peril they were about to face. This is, after all, the real purpose of prophecy in the first place. Prophecy is more than a message about of what will happen in the future, but a declaration of the mind of God that always has a moral purpose—to get us to change the way we are living.

In the light of this peril, Paul offers Timothy (and us) some sound pastoral advice on how to prepare for those days. First, Timothy must give careful attention to the study of the sacred Scriptures which he has known from infancy and which have prepared him for salvation in Christ (3:14-15). To underscore this Paul reminds him all Scripture is "inspired by God." In many modern translations the phrase 'inspired by God' is translated by the phrase "God-breathed," a more literal rendering of the Greek word. It simply means "to breathe out" as when a person exhales. Applied to God in this passage it means that God *exhaled* and the result was Scripture! The implications couldn't be clearer: Scripture is the only God-breathed book in the universe. That being the case, Timothy must build his entire life and ministry upon it.

In my library at my home I have many Christian books which I have collected through the years. I once brought my sons into my library to show them all of my books and to speak to them about the importance of reading. I told them how blessed we were to have so many Christian authors to inform us. But holding up my Bible, I reminded them that this book alone was "God-breathed." While I wanted them to develop a love for reading, I wanted them to always hold Sacred Scripture in the highest place.

Paul's exhortation to Timothy regarding Scripture is followed by his command that Timothy give due diligence to preaching the word

(II Timothy 4:1-2). It is not a coincidence that this follows what has previously been said about Scripture. Only where the full authority of Scripture is carefully maintained, can there be any real authority for preaching. The long history of the church bears this out. In those periods in church history where the highest view of Scripture was maintained, great preaching followed. Correspondingly, those periods when the church wavered regarding the nature of Scripture were times when great preaching was rare.

Looking at what Paul says about preaching, one thing is clear— Paul views preaching as the main occupation of a pastor. Timothy must be faithful to perform this task regardless of his emotional state ('instant in season and out of season') or whether it was welcomed ('the time will come when men will not endure sound doctrine'). When I taught from this passage in my series on II Timothy in our local church I dealt with what I called the 'peril of *evasion*'—evading the Gospel in an age when it's not popular. I examined all of the reasons that we evade sound teaching today to our own peril. This kind of apostolic urgency regarding preaching is desperately needed in the church today. We could only wish that more pastors approached the preaching task with this same level of apostolic urgency.

In the remainder of this chapter I want to examine three reasons for the loss of this urgency regarding preaching in the Church today. They are: the effect television and other visual media have had on preaching, the change in our basic views regarding pastoral ministry, and the replacement of biblical preaching with pulpiteering. A brief description of each follows.

The TV Generation and Preaching

Since television first appeared there have been numerous studies regarding its effects on those who watch. For the most part, these studies focus on the *content* of the shows aired; the fact that much of the programming on television is morally objectionable. What these studies did not measure, though, is that incessant television watching has a dulling effect on the mind. As viewers sit passively gazing at images on the screen, the mind is lulled into a passive state. Several generations have now watched the world go by rather than participated in it.

While I know of no study which has measured the impact television and other visual media has had on preaching, it stands to reason that preaching has suffered as well, due to incessant television watching. Since listening to the preached word requires the fullest use of the mental powers, it stands to reason that television has a direct effect on the ability of hearers to follow carefully reasoned arguments. When you take into account that television, movies, and the Internet are now the main ways most Americans get their news and information, it is not surprising that it has also effected preaching. According to George Barna, "one half of Americans are functionally illiterate; unable to read the Scripture with understanding and unable to comprehend the sermons we are preaching."

Concluding that it is better to capitulate than fight, many churches today have abandoned the traditional role of preaching for multimedia presentations and other means of getting the message out. The belief is that it really doesn't matter *how* people receive the message as long as they receive it. Yet those who believe that, overlook the fact that God has ordained not only the message but also the *means* by which people are to receive it—the "preached" word. The apostle Paul acknowledges that this is foolishness, but it is God's appointed means of getting the message out. Therefore it must never be abandoned, even if the culture deems it unacceptable (I Corinthians 1:18). That does not mean that we can't make use of technology or other things to assist us in our preaching. Still, we must always remember that preaching is God's means of promulgating the message. The reason God ordained preaching as the means of saving people is that sinful men and women need to be humbled if they are to be saved. And there is no more sure way of humbling sinners than by making it necessary to receive a message from a preacher! That means that as long as there are fallen human beings, there will be a need for someone to stand and proclaim the glorious truth of God's grace in Christ.

Pastors as Preachers

Another reason for the devaluing of preaching today is the change in how both people and pastors view pastoral ministry. Whereas preaching was once considered to be the most important task of pastoral ministry that is no longer the case. Many pastors now consider such tasks as counseling, administrating, and vision-casting to be more important than the task of proclaiming the glorious grace of the Gospel. The result has been disastrous for preaching in the Church. That's because those who have excelled at the preaching task have done so by making it their life's work, rather than a mere corollary.

A story in the book of Acts illustrates the importance of safeguarding preaching as the most important vocation of those called to the ministry. The Grecian widows were apparently being overlooked in the daily ministration of food, and the matter was brought to the apostles (Acts 6:1). There seems to have been an expectation for the apostles to become directly involved in this matter. This presented a real dilemma. Should the apostles leave off preaching the Word of God to take care of the legitimate needs of the Grecian widows, or should they delegate this task to others so as to give their undivided attention to the ministry of the Word? They wisely chose the latter, recognizing that their priority was to give themselves to the important task of preaching the Word of God (Acts 6:4).

Whenever I read this story I have put myself in the place of the apostles, asking whether or not I would have chosen as they had, especially knowing it might leave me vulnerable to the charge that I was partial to my own. I fear that in the early years of my ministry I would have made the wrong choice. If faced with this choice today though, I think I would choose more wisely. By God's grace, I think I have learned the necessity of carefully protecting my time so as to give adequate time to prepare for the ministry of the word.

This story in Acts has great relevance for pastors today who face the same pressure to give the priority of their time to tasks other than the preaching of the word. The wise pastor will deal with this temptation early in his ministry by learning to delegate to others those tasks not requiring his attention. But let the leader beware: Satan will resist tooth and nail anyone who decides to make preaching a priority! He (Satan) knows full well that it is only the Gospel and the preaching of the word that changes lives, and therefore he will do everything in his power to dissuade the leader intent on giving his attention to this all important task.

Yet it is not just pastors and leaders that must learn this, but church members as well. Members often view pastors primarily as as crisis counselors, encouragers, and administrators before they see them as preachers and teachers of God's word. That is why many of God's people receive their instruction outside their local church instead of first receiving it first from their local pastor and elders. This has greatly diminished the pastoral office. For God has ordained that pastors and elders be the main disseminators of biblical truth to the people of God.

I learned this the hard way in my first pastorate. Many of people in my church attended various meetings throughout the week where they would often hear strange teachings. When they came to church on Sunday they would challenge me for not teaching what they heard their favorite preacher teaching earlier that week. Instead of receiving divine truth from their local church and challenging everything else in the light of what their church was saying, they were challenging their local church having accepted at face value what they heard during the week. This is a perversion of God's order and greatly dishonors those who work hard at preaching and teaching (I Timothy 5:17).

Preachers or Pulpiteers

Earlier in this chapter I mentioned the failure to distinguish between preaching and *pulpiteering* as a major reason for the devaluing of preaching. Martyn Lloyd Jones used this term in his classic work on preaching (Preachers and Preaching) to describe those who use pulpits to stir people's emotions not so much by what they say, but by *how* they say it. This often passes for preaching in many churches today. I myself have sat under the ministry of trained *pulpiteers* who could hold entire audiences spellbound by the simple turn of a phrase.

It is important therefore to distinguish the difference between pulpiteering and preaching. The simplest way to distinguish between them is to say that preaching is *content*-driven while pulpiteering is *style*-driven. When a person is preaching it is not *how* he is saying a thing, but *what* he is saying that determines if he is preaching God's word. The goal of biblical preaching is to clearly *explain* the Word of God, and then apply it in such a way that people are forced to grapple with it. True preachers do not attempt to move people through manipulation and skilled oratory. They know that true transformation occurs only when biblical truth is understood and applied to the heart.

The apostle Paul is a great example of a biblical preacher, though by his own admission he was not a great orator (II Corinthians 10:10). It is often assumed that Paul admitted in this passage to having not been a good preacher, yet that is clearly not the case. He does admit in this passage that, at least by Hellenistic standards, he was not a great orator. Yet when it came to being a faithful minister of the cross of Christ, he actually viewed his lack of oratorical skills as an advantage rather than a hindrance. It safeguarded him from obscuring the message with wise and persuasive words (I Corinthians 1:17).

Most of those who are considered to be great preachers today are, for the most part, pulpiteers. Unfortunately, most have never had the privilege of sitting under gifted preachers of the Word. Pulpiteers abound in the Church today, especially when it comes to so-called *evangelistic* preaching. Instead of relying on the power of the Gospel, many evangelists today are trained in creating an atmosphere complete with soft music and constant reminders of what might happen if a person went out of a meeting and was struck by a car. When comparing this to great evangelistic preaching of the past such as that of John Wesley

144 A Passion for Truth

and George Whitfield during the Great Awakening, the difference is
palpable. These men preached messages rich in biblical content that
were aimed at convincing their hearers of the *truth* of the Gospel.

The fact that biblical preaching is content-driven rather than
style-driven does not mean that style is not important when one is
preaching biblical messages. It was said of George Whitfied that if he
had not become a preacher of the Gospel, he would have been one
of the greatest stage actors of his day. The difference though is that
Whitfield's messages were not mere emotional appeals, like that of
many modern pulpiteers today, but rather were packed with biblical
theology. Their aim was not simply to appeal to the emotions, but to
educate the mind so that the hearers were convinced of the truth. At
the same time, Whitfield knew how to use emotion and passion to the
fullest when preaching the Gospel.

One preacher who was a shining example of great evangelistic preaching was the nineteenth century English preacher, Charles
Spurgeon. Over the many years that Spurgeon occupied the pulpit of
Metropolitan Tabernacle, he never gave what would be considered a
traditional altar call. Nevertheless, thousands attributed their conversion to Spurgeon's ministry during the years of his London pastorate.
While always preaching biblical messages in the pulpit on Sunday, he
interviewed those each week who were under conviction of sin as a
result of listening to his sermons. While Spurgeon was not afraid to
show emotion when he preached, his sermons were far more than a
flare for the dramatic. Spurgeon possessed great natural oratorical skill
but it was always subservient to his overwhelming passion—to preach
the Word of God in such a way that sinners might be converted.

Sadly, much preaching today is evaluated by the excitement it
generates rather than its faithfulness to Scripture. Many Christians
expect preachers to be entertainers or great storytellers rather than
expounders of God's Word. Yet true preaching is always judged by
its faithfulness to the Word of God and the Gospel, not the entertainment value that is derived from it. To judge preachers by such a

worldly standard is to greatly devalue preaching and in the end, does a great disservice to the Church of God.

Pastors as Teachers

In a previous chapter I mentioned the Puritan belief that true preaching contains both "light" and "heat" (knowledge of God presented in the power of the Spirit). By "light" the Puritans essentially meant that preaching is always first and foremost *theological*. The preacher assumes he is speaking to those who need to know something about God and themselves that they are not presently in possession of. So before the preacher is anything else (pastor, counselor, arbiter) he is a *theologian*. He may not have a degree in theology from a seminary, but the very fact that he has something vital to say about God constitutes him as a theologian. When he rises to speak, he has studied the Word of God and can therefore speak with divine authority—an authority that is not derived from an office but from Holy Scripture.

Reading the sermons of some of the great preachers throughout church history confirms that true preaching is theological in nature. These sermons reveal a depth of understanding of Scripture which is rare to find in the Church today. Those who preached them worked hard to ensure that their preaching was solidly rooted in Scripture. It is said of Spurgeon that he read five books a week and Jonathan Edwards spent twelve to fourteen hours a day in his study. It would be easy to conclude that these men were shirking their pastoral responsibilities by spending such exorbitant amounts of time alone in study. Yet they did so precisely because they believed that they could not give to others what they themselves did not have. For this reason, their ministries were powerful in converting the lost and building up the church of God.

The practice of an Edwards or a Spurgeon seems strange to the average pastor today who spends the majority of his time counseling, administrating programs, and being a motivational speaker. Even pastors who desire to pursue biblical and theological studies find very little time for such pursuits in the modern church. Most pastors today struggle to find adequate time for sermon preparation let alone for deeper theological study. It is only as pastors view the preaching and teaching of God's Word as their primary task that they are apt to make the time necessary to gain efficiency in handling the Word of truth.

Over the years, I have made it my aim to study great preachers of past ages so as to learn all that I could about preaching. While this exercise has been most blessed to my soul, it also has been quite humbling. After reading a Spurgeon sermon it is easy to feel like you have never really preached a good sermon at all! Nevertheless, I have found the study of these preachers to be a source of great encouragement. They have spurred me to believe that through much diligence, I could become a better preacher.

Expository Preaching

Not only must the preacher be diligently prepared theologically, he must also be committed to *expository* teaching and preaching. Even a cursory reading of church history will reveal that preachers committed to the regular exposition of Scripture have been the most successful. Why? Because expository preaching is preaching which grounds the message in a particular passage (or passages) of Scripture rather than in the preacher's own thoughts. When preachers draw their message from Scripture it carries the authority of God Himself, it being an exposition of God's own thoughts. All *true* preaching therefore is expository in nature.

There are a number of common misunderstandings people have when it comes to understanding expository preaching. A major one is the idea that a sermon is expository when it deals with a several texts in the message rather than just one. But the number of texts a preacher uses does not determine whether a sermon is expository. What makes a message expository is that the sermon is based solidly in the text(s) rather than in the thoughts and ideas of the preacher. When a man rises to preach it is not his personal opinions or his subjective experiences we are interested in, rather what God has spoken in Scripture. God may certainly use the preacher's unique experiences, but what gives the message power is the fact that it has behind it the authority of God's Word itself.

I often meet with indifference whenever I have opportunity to speak to pastors about the benefits of expository preaching. Some will tell me that they previously sat under expository preaching in the past and found it boring. When I ask them what made the preaching they listened to expository they usually point to the fact that the message referenced a number of Scriptures or that there were several obscure Hebrew and Greek words used which few understood. No wonder they found it boring! If that is what expository preaching is I would have found it boring as well. Thankfully, the fact that the preacher references obscure Greek or Hebrew words is not what makes a message expository.

Those who think that expository preaching is boring should read (or listen) to great expositors of the past such as Dr. Martyn Lloyd Jones, pastor of Westminster Cathedral in London in the twentieth century. The first thing that strikes you when reading a Lloyd Jones' sermon is the richness of the biblical content. Yet those who sat under his ministry would tell you that his sermons were far from boring. Even a cursory reading of one of the Doctors' sermons demonstrates the passion and pathos with which he faithfully expounded the Word of God.

Preaching: Igniting Passion for Truth

My purpose in this chapter was not to provide a crash course in homiletics (the science of preaching). Rather, it was to call attention to the fact that God has always used preaching as a major means of igniting passion for truth in the people of God. When preachers accurately and faithfully expound the Scriptures, it produces great respect for the Word of God so that people begin to treat it seriously. This alone should convince pastors to become skilled expositors of God's Word.

While preaching is certainly not the only means of igniting passion for truth, it is a major one. The careful, God-drenched, anointed exposition of a holy man of God will have a deep effect on a congregation over an extended period of time. That is why the apostle Paul told Timothy that he should honor elders who "work hard at preaching and teaching" (I Timothy 5:17, NASB). Those who are privileged to sit under such pastors and teachers should honor them by carefully listening to their biblical expositions.

I am convinced that, were there more of this kind of preaching in the Church today, there would also be a greater passion for truth among the people of God. I am also convinced that preaching itself would once again be elevated to the place it held in previous ages. The church of God desperately needs this type of preaching. Our congregations are starved for the truth of God from God-exalting expositors, passionate about expounding it. Many have been spiritually emaciated by pulpiteers who, while keeping them excited, have not fed them from the rich pasturelands of God's word. There is a cry throughout the land today for a new company of preachers to arise who will not flinch from their God-called task of proclaiming the truth to a generation desperate for a clear word from God. May God hasten the day when the church of God is filled with such God-exalting expositors of His Word! Amen.

CHAPTER TEN

Truth is a Person

Throughout this book I have attempted to dispel the notion that believers must choose between the passionate pursuit of God Himself and passion for truth. I have tried to make the case that the passionate pursuit of God also includes the passionate pursuit of divine truth as well. The choice for the spiritual Christian is never between the development of the brain at the expense of the heart. Both are essential to authentic Christian living.

In this final chapter though I want to sound a note of caution. It is one I mentioned briefly in a previous chapter but now feel compelled to focus squarely upon. It is that intellectual apprehension of propositional truth should never be construed as knowledge of God Himself. While knowledge of truth is essential to a proper knowledge of God, it must always be coupled with personal, experiential knowledge of God. Therefore, in the pursuit of genuine Christian spirituality, believers are to grow both in knowledge of objective truth as well as in personal knowledge of God gained through subjective experience.

We must never forget, therefore, that knowing the Bible and knowing God are not the same thing. Failure to realize this has led to gross imbalance in the lives of many Christians. Those who emphasize the experiential side of Christian living focus on personal experiences as the way to gain personal knowledge of God. Yet they often fail to realize that without real and substantial knowledge of Scripture, there can be no true knowledge of God. On the other hand, those who emphasize the importance of biblical knowledge often forget that without a corresponding emphasis on experiential knowledge, their knowledge of God may be largely theoretical.

In this chapter I want to focus on the latter error—mistaking Bible knowledge for knowledge of God Himself. I have personally learned that intellectual knowledge of God gained through the study of the Scriptures, if not coupled with personal, experiential knowledge of God Himself, will not yield a knowledge of the holy. After my initial conversion, God gave me an insatiable desire to learn Holy Scripture. I spent almost every waking moment reading and meditating upon its precepts. At the same time, God led me through some very painful experiences which at first I didn't understand. Eventually, I learned that it was not only personal knowledge of Scripture, but also personal dealings *with* God which would lead me to a true knowledge of God. In no way did this mean that it wasn't important for me to study God's word, but that I must always be careful to avoid the temptation to separate intellectual knowledge of God from the pursuit of God Himself.

There are some believers today who view spirituality as simply a matter of accumulating biblical knowledge and theological information. They recite the creeds and are orthodox when it comes to their beliefs, convinced that possession of such knowledge is what makes them spiritual. Yet they fail to recognize that the real purpose of theological knowledge is to cultivate the passionate pursuit of God Himself. In his classic work *The Pursuit of God*, A.W. Tozer warned of the dangers of mistaking orthodoxy for passion for God Himself. He encouraged his readers to move beyond mere doctrinal apprehension to real experience with God.

Dr. Tozer was undoubtedly addressing typical churchgoers who equated commitment to orthodoxy as evidence of spirituality. An ardent student of church history, he believed that true saints in every age were those who pursued God passionately. He fought vigorously against the idea that correct theology *alone* was all that was needed to cultivate Christian spirituality. We should take Dr. Tozer's warning seriously and shun a faith void of corresponding experience with God.

In seeking to counter the subjective tendencies running rampant in the church today it is not necessary that we adopt an 'experience-less' Christianity as the alternative. Such a faith is no more biblical than one based *solely* in experience. The biblical writers were all men of rich experience with God who both knew Him as well as knew *of* Him. Being well taught and grounded in the truth of God should lead us to desire all that Scripture sets forth as normative for Christian living. We will not shun any valid spiritual experience, knowing that it is an important component of Christian spirituality.

You Search the Scriptures

How can we be passionate pursuers of truth without losing passion for God Himself? The place to start is by recognizing that *truth* in Scripture is not only the sum total of biblical revelation, but a *Person*—the Lord Jesus Christ (John 14:6). In practical terms, that means that the truth of Scripture should *always* lead us to the reality of the Lord Jesus Christ Himself. Learning the Word of God is not merely a matter of mastering certain biblical subjects such as such as salvation, discipleship, prayer, humility, fasting, etc. Rather, it is learning Christ (Ephesians 4:20). God never intended that Scripture become an end in itself, but a means by which we gain *real* knowledge of the Lord Jesus.

A story in John's Gospel illustrates this well. After Jesus had healed the lame man at the pool of Bethesda, the Pharisees persecuted him for healing on the Sabbath (John 5). In one of the longest discourses in John's Gospel, the Lord defends his action by declaring that He was only doing what the Father was doing at that time (5:17). Towards the end of the discourse, the Lord deals with the Pharisees attitude towards Scripture. He acknowledged their love for Scripture evidenced by their fastidious study of it ('you search the Scriptures'), yet indicts them for failing to recognize the real purpose for which the Scriptures were given: as the means of revealing the Messiah! (5:39). Rather than being a means to an end, they had made the study of Scripture an end in itself and in so doing, reduced the Bible to little more than an elaborate rule-book instead of a book which reveals the Ruler.

Ancient Pharisees are not the only ones that have this problem. We also can use the Bible in such a way so as to fail to realize why it was given. The only way to avoid this error, is by making sure that when we are studying the Bible, we are always relating it to the Person of the Lord Jesus and His redemptive work. We must never allow our Bible study to be a mere academic exercise. All knowledge of Scripture, therefore, must be subordinated to our overall quest for greater and greater personal knowledge of God and Christ.

In Luke's account of the resurrection (Luke 24), the Lord Jesus appears to the eleven apostles and opens their minds so that they could understand the "things concerning Himself in the Scriptures" (24:44-45). As they listened to the Lord Jesus expound the Scriptures that day, an entirely new world opened up to them! Those same Scriptures which they had known from childhood, now revealed to them a living Person rather than theological topics. When Luke tells us that the Lord Jesus opened their minds to understand the Scriptures, he does not mean that He found it necessary to reacquaint them with their Old Testament. These men were Jews and had no need for Jesus to tell them again about such things as the flood of Noah, the call of Abraham, and Moses at the burning bush, since they had grown up with these stories. What they needed was a total *reinterpretation* of that history with Messiah now as the center. That is what the Lord gave them in the Upper Room. He provided them with an interpretive key by which these same Scriptures they had known from childhood became a living document rather than mere letters written on papyrus.

Theologians often distinguish the Bible from Christ by using the designation 'God's Word written' as distinguished from 'God's Word *incarnate*' (John 1:14). Most people today, when hearing the term "Word" automatically assume it is a reference to the Bible. Yet in John's writings Jesus is referred to as the 'Word of God' (John 1:1, Revelation 19:13). When believers in the first century heard that term they would not have thought of Scripture first but of God's Word *Incarnate*—Jesus Christ. That doesn't mean that they had a low view of Scripture, for in point of fact they held the highest view of God's Word written. Its just that for them, God's Word was not primarily a book, but a Person.

All study of Scripture therefore should be a quest to find the living Christ within its pages. Only in this manner can we avoid the tendency to divorce the written Word from the living Word. In one of his books, Oswald Chambers warned of the unreality that comes from divorcing the *words* of God (Scripture) from the *Word* of God (Person). He went as far as to say that in the end it produces *antichrist*; an authority other than Christ Himself. Experience has proven this to be true.

The Problem of Legalism

One of the deadliest spiritual maladies resulting from divorcing Scripture from Christ is *legalism*. It a spiritual cancer that constitutes one of the greatest problems in the Body of Christ today. It not only rears its ugly head when tradition and human rules are substituted for biblical truth, but also when Christian orthodoxy is understood and taught. Simply spoken, when knowing the Bible is stressed apart from knowing Christ, legalism often results.

We often forget that the New Testament itself may be handled in the same way that the Pharisees handled the Law of Moses. Whether arguing over a certain form of baptism or the keeping of certain days, many believers today reduce the New Testament to principles to be obeyed and in the process, miss entirely the spirit of *grace* which has come in Christ. They fail to realize that extracting principles from Scripture without an understanding of God's grace tends to lead to a tendency to view these principles as 'stepping-stones' to the kingdom (if you do them you are blessed, if you don't you are cursed). Without realizing it people begin to rely on perfect obedience to the principles of Scripture rather than the grace of God. And this is the essence of legalism.

As a new believer, I once attended a seminar taught by a very popular Bible teacher who specialized in this type of 'principled' approach to teaching Scripture. His specialty was to teach on the principle of submission to authority. In the seminar, he spoke eloquently about the need for children to submit to their parents even going as far as to say that a man should not go into Christian ministry unless he first had the blessing of his parents. As I listened, I realized I had never obtained my parents' blessing to go into the ministry (I never thought to ask my Jewish parents if they wanted their son to be a Christian minister) so I concluded that I had no right to be in the ministry and should therefore look for another vocation. Thanks to the counsel of godly men, I soon realized that God does, at times, call people to do things even parents may not approve of. That was the case when Jesus remained behind in Jerusalem to teach the doctors and scribes in the temple during the Passover feast (Luke 2:41-51). I soon learned that I must never apply the principles of Scripture to myself or others in a way that enslaves people.

While obedience to what the Scriptures teach is important, we should never think that our relationship with God rests *solely* on our perfect obedience. To do so is to reduce the Christian life to obedience to principles rather than relying on the grace of God. One of the reasons we so easily gravitate to living by principles is that it is our default mode as sinners. We naturally gravitate towards law unless we are instructed in the grace of God. Besides our inherent nature, it is also what we learned as children—that God rewards good behavior and punishes bad behavior. Do you remember when you were little and your mom or dad told you that God rewards good little girls and boys? The inference is, if you are not good you will miss out on the blessing.

When we apply this to God we think that God can only bless us when we're 'good.' And that's just the problem—we are not 'good' and therefore (in our minds) forfeit the blessing. To live this way is to live a 'performance-based life,' a far cry from that obedience which is the result of a heart changed by the grace of God. Whenever performance is substituted for obedience it inevitably produces frustrated people who are trying to earn favor with God.

Finding Scripture's Grace Connection

The only way to avoid legalism in our handling of God's Word is to seek to relate all of Scripture to the redemptive work of Jesus Christ. As stated earlier, when studying any passage of God's Word we must always seek to relate it to the grace which has come in Christ. This is to use Scripture as God intended—as a means of illuminating our hearts to all that God in Christ has accomplished for us (II Timothy 3:15). Failing to relate Scripture to God's finished work in Christ makes the Bible an end in itself instead of a means by which we are gaining knowledge of Christ.

The best way to view Scripture is to see it as a written record of salvation-history. The story of the Old Testament is the story of the calling into being of a nation called *Israel* with the express purpose of preparing them to as God's chosen vessel through which the Messiah would come. Sadly, that is not how most people in the church today have been taught to view it. Either they completely allegorize so it has little or no meaning, or else they reduce it to little more than a book which teaches certain moral stories like the faith of Abraham, the courage of David, and the faithfulness of Daniel, etc. When reading the Old Testament it is certainly true that these things may be gleaned from it. Still, we miss entirely the purpose for which the Old Testament was given when we reduce it to little more than a book containing a few moral stories or a few extant prophecies concerning the Messiah. What is desperately needed today is to teach people to view it as Jesus taught his disciples— as a covenantal document revealing the coming of the kingdom of God and the redemptive work of Jesus the Messiah (Luke 24).

The same is true in our handling of the New Testament. It is important to remember that the New Testament was not first a written document, but a covenant mediated to human hearts by the Spirit of God (II Corinthians 3:6). It would be several years after Pentecost before it would actually be written. Nevertheless, even before it was written it was in full force as a covenant. To forget that is to run the risk of turning it into a rule-book. Sadly, this is exactly what many in the body of Christ today have done.

A Passion for Christ the Truth

Throughout this book, I have sounded out the theme that passion for God must include the passionate pursuit of truth as well. Since Jesus referred to Himself as the *truth* (John 14:6), passion for truth is nothing less than a passion for Jesus Christ. We don't have to choose therefore between passion for God and passion for truth since both are integral aspects of true Christian spirituality.

To become a disciple one must "believe in Jesus." This is infinitely more than merely believing certain things *about* Him, but believing *into* Him. We are to believe in Jesus Christ Himself—born of a virgin, crucified, risen, and seated at the right hand of God from which He now rules the universe. This is the essence of true faith. Jesus did not leave his followers with the option of believing in his teachings, while disbelieving the claims He made for Himself.

Over the years, I have met certain individuals who professed to believe that Jesus was a great teacher, yet rejected His claim to be the Messiah. I have pointed out to them the inconsistency of their position. If they claim to believe He was a great teacher than they would believe He was the Messiah for that is exactly what He claimed to be (John 4:26). At that point most of them begin to fudge. They realize that they cannot have it both ways: Either what He taught was wrong, in which case He was not a good teacher, or else what He taught is true, in which case they should fall down and worship Him. There is no other alternative.

When we come to know Christ as the embodiment of truth, the words of Scripture begin to have the same effect on our hearts and minds that Jesus' own words had on the two on the road to Emmaus (Luke 24:32). Their hearts burned as Jesus opened up the Scriptures to them. As we begin to hear Jesus Himself speak to us again through Scripture, our own hearts begin to burn with passion for God. This is how we should study the Bible. Studying the Bible merely to gain information, instead of hearing the Lord speak to us may actually hinder more than help. It is possible to learn of such things as the Tabernacle in the Wilderness, Solomon's temple, tithing, the millennium, and many other things, yet learn nothing of Christ and the grace He offers. To discover the truth of Scripture we must go beyond merely collecting information and learn to relate all we read to Christ and His saving work. Failing to do so may lead us to become like those the apostle Paul described who are "ever learning and never able to come to the knowledge of the truth" (II Timothy 3:7).

There is a great difference therefore between being *Bible* taught and *Spirit* taught. The Holy Spirit's main role is to disclose to the believer a personal knowledge of the Christ of history. To accomplish this, He uses the truth of Scripture but that truth must never become an end in itself. If we want a passion for Christ therefore we must not only study the Scriptures but pray that the Spirit reveals Christ to our hearts as we learn what Scripture teaches (see Ephesians 1:15-18).

Even though we may have initially come to know God's Son by an operation of the Spirit, the Spirit *always* leads us to Scripture so that our faith might be grounded in truth, rather than our own subjective impressions. Passionate Christians therefore are *both* Bible taught and Spirit taught. They feel no need to choose between them knowing that both are essential in the development of the passionate heart. Instead of reading the Bible as a rule book, they read it as a revelation of the Son of God whom they have come to personally know. For them, Scripture is the vehicle through which the living Christ is revealed. This enables them to develop a passion for God's Word written, as well as God's Word incarnate. Both constitute normative Christian spirituality.

CPSIA information can be obtained at www.ICGtesting.com
Printed in the USA
LVOW05s0327270714

396162LV00001B/9/P